Victor
PUBLISHING
victorpublishing.co.uk

Daydreams
& NIGHTMARES

**MILLWALL FOOTBALL CLUB
IN THE 2000s
Part One**

Merv Payne

First published in Great Britain in 2022
Copyright © Merv Payne 2022
Published by Victor Publishing - victorpublishing.co.uk

Merv Payne has asserted his right under the Copyright, Designs and Patents Act 1988 to be identified as the author of this work.

All rights reserved. No part of this publication may be reproduced, distributed, or transmitted in any form or by any means, including photo-copying, recording, or other electronic or mechanical methods, without the prior written permission of the author.

Every reasonable effort has been made to trace copyright holders of material reproduced in this book, but if any have been inadvertently overlooked, the author would be glad to hear from them.

ISBN: 9798846803923

Victor
PUBLISHING
victorpublishing.co.uk

Contents

Introduction		11
Season 99-00	**The Same Old Song**	**15**
Chapter 1	*Moving, but going nowhere*	17
Chapter 2	*So close, you can touch it*	25
Chapter 3	*The old enemy returns*	37
Season 00-01	**Cheer Up**	**47**
Chapter 4	*Tough love*	49
Chapter 5	*A new broom*	63
Chapter 6	*Beware the sides of March*	79
Chapter 7	*Daydream believers*	83
Season 01-02	**We Can Be Heroes**	**93**
Chapter 8	*Perspective*	95
Chapter 9	*Palace, Palace, who the*	103
Chapter 10	*Insult & injury*	115
Chapter 11	*Here we go again*	123
Season 02-03	**Hangover**	**131**
Chapter 12	*Damage limitation*	133
Chapter 13	*A Sads ending*	145
Season 03-04	**A Dish Best Served Cold**	**153**
Chapter 14	*Everything's changing*	155
Chapter 15	*Wise after the event*	165
Chapter 16	*Never saw that coming*	171
Chapter 17	*We're all going on a European tour*	181
Chapter 18	*Four is the magic number*	189
Season 04-05	**End of an Era**	**201**
Chapter 19	*Fifteen minutes of fame*	203
Chapter 20	*An offer you can't refuse*	213
Chapter 21	*Up the creek*	219

introduction

Daydreams & Nightmares - Millwall FC in the 2000s - Part 1

In case you missed it...

Here's the story so far. Forgive me if that sounds like the cheesey intro to a television sit-com, but let's not kid ourselves, it's a pretty fitting description for Millwall Football Club most of the time. So here goes...

When you were last with us, Millwall had ended the 1990s - the 20th century even - by making a little bit of history. Unfortunately it wasn't the sort of history that Lions fans had perhaps dreamed of as they went into the 90s. I mean it would have been nice if Millwall had taken the honour of being the only Premier League team still to remain undefeated at home in 1999 for example.

Sadly, that top flight dreamboat had long since set sail. Millwall meanwhile had run aground, been marooned back in the Third Division and almost sunk by administration.

So they had to settle for the very Millwall-like honour of being the team that scored the last English League goal of the 20th century.

Dave Livermore's late, late winner in the thrilling 3-2 win at The Den over Brentford (whatever happened to them?) made for a happy Hogmanay for Lions fans - and eternal fame for Livers. Pedants - as pedants do (and there are none more fastidious than the football variety) tried to take this dubious honour away from Livermore with various different definitions of what constitutes the last goal of the century but to go into that would deprive both player - and club - of an all-too-rare accolade so let's leave it at that.

That century-ending drama saw Millwall sat nicely placed for a challenge for promotion to get the new millennium off to the perfect start. They had finally found a management team that worked, and after repeating the same old mistakes made in the 80s during the 90s when youth was sacrificed to pay the bills and over-age overpaid space-fillers that turned out to be time-wasters brought in to the club's demise, there was now a thriving youth system that was already bearing fruit and astute recruitment had built a solid, exciting side.

The time was right, the time was now. After ten years of barren, promotionless seasons, everything was about to fall into place.

What could possibly go wrong?

Daydreams & Nightmares - Millwall FC in the 2000s - Part 1

Daydreams & Nightmares - Millwall FC in the 2000s - Part 1

the same old song...
99/00

Daydreams & Nightmares - Millwall FC in the 2000s - Part 1

1. Moving, but going nowhere

January 2000...
1 January - Millennium celebrations take place throughout the UK. The Millennium Dome in London is officially opened by HM The Queen; 31 January - Dr. Harold Shipman is sentenced to life imprisonment after being found guilty of murdering fifteen patients in Greater Manchester between 1995 and 1998; The Manic Street Preachers reach number one with their single The Masses Against The Classes, sandwiched by Westlife and Britney Spears in the first charts of the new century...

Newton's third law famously states: for every action, there is an equal and opposite reaction. Just days into the New Year which had been set up so perfectly by that late win against Brentford and seen Millwall consolidate a handy fourth place in the table, The Lions decided to abandon all plans of a promotion push and instead use the often tricky trip to Gigg Lane, Bury to illustrate Newton's wise words through the medium of football.

At a venue where Millwall rarely enjoyed success, there was little surprise to the hardy travelling Lions faithful that had endured the bitter north west conditions when they supped their half time Bovril having seen their team 1-0 behind courtesy of a Reid goal in first half injury time.

There was the first bit. Conceding right on half time will have, in Newton's wisdom, levelled up that last gasp winner at The Den days before.

But then, in the second half, Millwall sought to explode this scientific theory by launching an unexpected comeback - just has Brentford had done. I'm not sure if that favours Newton or not, I'm getting a bit confused by it all if I'm honest.

A neat Neil Harris goal ten minutes after the restart switched the momentum of the match Millwall's way and, with just ten minutes remaining, Paul Ifill grabbed what looked like the winner.

But just as Brentford fans felt they had scooped the late spoils, Millwall's celebrations of back to back victories was scuppered deep into injury time with a 96th minute leveller for Bury by Redmond.

It was one of those occasions when a draw felt as bad as a defeat, even though The Lions probably would have taken a point at half time,

Millwall had been in fourth place in the table since their 2-1 win at Wycombe Wanderers five games before, and were still in that same fourth place when The Chairboys visited for the return match at The Den four days later.

But frustrations abound once more as Millwall were unable to take advantage of mid-table Wycombe and complete the double to put pressure on the top two places.

Ex-Lion Sean Devine gave Lawrie Sanchez's side a 13th-minute lead which was cancelled out before half time by the increasingly lethal Neil Harris, but despite facing ten men for half of the second period, Millwall were worryingly short of ideas and all too easy for Wycombe to repel. Another draw, but still fourth in the table. Promotion is of course built on good home form, something that is pretty much ingrained in Millwall's history and that managerial duo Stevens and McLeary had made the bedrock of their tenure. Up until that disappointing Wycombe stalemate, The Lions were on a roll of four home wins on the spin with just one Den defeat so far that season - against promotion favourites Preston. The fact that this was their fifth draw in 13 home league matches said a lot about why they were struggling to make an impact on those top two automatic promotion spots.

Luck of course also plays a part and typically, as was becoming increasingly the case against one particular opponent, it deserted them for their next match.

Wigan had been installed as out and out favourites to win promotion now that Dave Whelan's millions were starting to reap their rewards. After somewhat fortunately beating The Lions at Wembley in the Auto Windscreens Shield final the previous season, heavy summer investment in their squad and a brand new purpose-built stadium had the previously unfashionable little football club surviving in a staunch rugby league town vying for popularity and dominance against its egg-shaped ball rival.

At the start of the season Wigan's expensively-assembled side had blown Millwall away, streaking into a 3-0 lead in the opening league match at The Den. A spirited fightback to draw the match 3-3 showed that perhaps the low-budget Lions weren't that far behind the free-spending title favourites, and just seven points separated table-topping Wigan from fourth-placed Millwall when the sides met at the JJB Stadium.

The day didn't get off to the best of starts when a bridge fire meant 200 travelling fans missed their train out of Euston and couldn't make the match. Also absent were key players in the injured Neil Harris, Marc Bircham and Tony Warner as well as the suspended Steven Reid and Lucas Neill who was on international duty.

To face the league leaders with basically a half strength side and come away with a point was testimony to the grit and determination that Stevens and McLeary had instilled in their team, but both players, management and fans must have spent that long journey home wondering what a full strength team could have done when Livermore gave them the lead early in the second half - only to be pegged back with 20 minutes left to leave The Lions with a third consecutive draw going into the crucial next home game with Stoke, and still in fourth place:

Nationwide League Division 2 - January 22nd 2000							
	P	W	D	L	F	A	PTS
1. Wigan	26	15	10	1	48	22	55
2. Bristol Rovers	26	16	5	5	38	21	53
3. Preston	25	15	7	3	43	21	52
4. Millwall	**27**	**13**	**9**	**5**	**42**	**29**	**48**
5. Stoke	26	13	8	5	38	23	47
6. Burnley	25	12	8	5	34	22	44

Despite the continued absence of Harris, Millwall were finally able to get their first win of the new century on the board courtesy of a first half goal from veteran striker Michael Gilkes.

Another striker, this one making a permanent exit from The Den was Danny Hockton who it had been announced had left the club for Conference outfit Stevenage Borough.

The contrast in fortunes of Hockton and the other young striker that had made the breakthrough into Billy Bonds' initial Millwall side back in 1997 was stark.

Richard Sadlier came on as a substitute in the win over Stoke and was quickly cementing his place in The Lions' strikeforce alongside Neil Harris and the other veteran frontmen in their squad: Paul Moody and Paul Shaw.

Hockton had looked the better prospect when both he and Sadlier formed that youthful frontline partnership under Bonds but a terrible run of injuries meant that, in the two and a half years since he'd made that first team bow, Hockton had managed to play in just 36 league matches for the club, most coming as sub, with four goals to show.

With a maximum finally under their belts, hopes were high as Millwall travelled to struggling Chesterfield for the last match in January.

The second-bottom Spirites had mustered just three wins all season and although Millwall travelled to the town of the crooked spire still without Harris and Neill, they would surely be too strong for a side in woeful form with just one win in their last 21 outings dating back to early September.

There was a certain amount of inevitability then about the way Chesterfield eased to a 2-0 victory in horrendous conditions. As gale-force winds and torrential rain lashed across the iconic little Saltergate stadium, Millwall barely managed a shot or attack of note in one of their feeblest submissions in many a year, quite out of character with the way Stevens and McLeary had shaped the team in their brief tenure.

It was a particularly inopportune time for another product of the Millwall youth system to make his first team bow.

Byron Bubb had been earning rave reviews persuading Stevens and McLeary to name him as one of the substitutes.

It's unlikely that either of the Lions' experienced managerial team would have been so presumptuous to assume that the match would be an easy introduction for new blood to be tested, but even they must have been shocked at how easily their opponents consolidated a first half goal. The second half introduction of Bubb can have done nothing for the youngster's confidence as Chesterfield secured the points with another seven minutes from time. Although the rain-soaked walk back to the dressing room via the tunnel directly beneath the furious travelling supporters will have certainly been character-building.

Chesterfield would go on to register just three more wins that season, finishing bottom of the table with a woeful 36 points - four of which had been taken off Millwall who had been unable to beat them in either of the league meetings. It was a familiar story throughout The Lions' history where so often the team was able to raise its game for the big matches as they had done seven days earlier at home to Stoke, but fall woefully short when expected to win.

The fact that little mention was made of the Chesterfield debacle in Alan McLeary's programme notes spoke volumes. Usually so honest and openly apologetic, both Rhino and Macca, being time-served Millwall servants, will have no doubt read the room and realised it was not time for words, but actions.

The first match of February proved a bitter-sweet affair. The return of Neil Harris saw a return to winning ways with a last-minute Paul Shaw penalty snatching a 1-0 win over mid-table Oldham, but the day was soured with the news that Harris would once again be missing for a spell. This time not through injury but a three match ban for a straight red card.

Harris had a rush of blood when fouled by Oldham's Mark Hotte in the 29th minute, and after an angry reaction from Harris which led to a pitch melee, referee Tony Bates decided to show the red card to Harris and just a yellow to the initial Oldham offender.

Off the pitch the club announced an impressive new acquisition in the shape of Ray Harford. The highly-respected coach was brought in, initially until the end of the season, to replace the outgoing David Kemp who had left to take up a similar role at Portsmouth. Harford had of course, just five years previously, assisted Kenny Dalglish at Blackburn Rovers when they won The Premier League title.

After spending ten weeks in fourth place another meek 0-2 defeat away, this time to another struggling side in Reading, really had the alarm bells ringing.

This league really was there for the taking with no one team taking it by the scruff of the neck. Early pacesetters Wigan were in the middle of an eight game winless run and a very ordinary Bristol Rovers side had taken over at the top. Millwall's worrying propensity of drawing at home and losing away was genuinely costing them a chance of automatic promotion.

Bournemouth were the next visitors to The Den on a day when the club announced another new arrival - this time to the playing staff.

Belgian winger Christophe Kinet had been snapped up from Strasbourg for a fee of £75,000. The 24-year-old's debut was delayed by, of all things, an unreliable courier who failed to get his international clearance papers delivered as promised.

Mid-table Bournemouth arrived with an impressive squad. The highly-rated young defender Eddie Howe accompanied at the back by Manchester United loanee John O'Shea, and livewire striker Mark Stein who always seemed to enjoy playing against Millwall.

In what would be the first of three more Harris-less matches, Millwall desperately needed to find goals from somewhere.

Fortunately they did, and two goals from Sadlier along with a last-minute Ifill strike gave The Lions their first three-goal return since that history-making victory over Brentford at the end of the previous year.

It was a victory that ended up looking far more comfortable than it actually was, with O'Shea giving The Cherries a third-minute lead. There was a distinct air of *"Here we go again"* around The Den, but fortunately Sadlier was on hand to level things up before the atmosphere became too toxic and played into the visitors' hands.

That somewhat fortuitous victory appeared to galvanise the side and two Paul Moody goals had the points wrapped up within the first 22 minutes in the next win away at rock-bottom Cambridge.

Finally Millwall seemed to have found that killer instinct and the ability to see off the struggling sides as well those who posed a promotion threat.

Now, with the crucial final two full months of the season looming, Millwall looked to be hitting form just at the right time:

Nationwide League Division 2 - February 28th 2000	P	W	D	L	F	A	PTS
1. Bristol Rovers	32	20	6	6	55	26	66
2. Preston	31	18	9	4	54	28	63
3. Millwall	**33**	**17**	**12**	**7**	**49**	**34**	**60**
4. Wigan	31	15	13	3	50	26	58
5. Burnley	31	16	10	5	43	25	58
6. Stoke	33	15	14	9	44	33	54

2. So close you can touch it...

March 2000...
2 March - The UK deports Augusto Pinochet to his native Chile where he will face trial for human rights violations; 31 March - Myra Hindley, who has spent 34 years in prison for her role in the Moors murders, loses a third High Court appeal against a Home Office ruling that her life sentence should mean life; Oasis reach number one for the fourth time with Go Let It Out...

The Grand National was just around the corner. This iconic race would no doubt bring its usual drama of early pacesetters streaking ahead, only to fade or fall before the finish line. The eventual victors would be those thoroughbreds who had the experience and shrewd jockey skills to stay just in touch with the leaders and hit the front at the perfect moment, racing to glory, uncatchable in the home straight. This had to be Millwall's strategy now. Their final 13 fixtures included matches against Bristol Rovers, Preston and Burnley and would be a true test of their promotion credentials. The other ten were against teams with little or nothing to play for, although they tend to be the toughest nuts to crack.

The first of those ten opponents who seemingly had

nothing to fear from below not much hope of troubling the play-off contenders was Bristol City. So often a thorn in Millwall's side, The Lions started March at The Den in stunning style with goals from Cahill (2) and Ifill putting them 3-0 up by the half hour mark. Another Sadlier strike early in the second half put the gloss on a fine 4-1 win - but had they started to hit the front too soon?

The excitement of a promotion-winning run-in similar to that seen in 1976 and 1988 was palpable three days later when, back at The Den, struggling Scunthorpe were the visitors. The Iron had managed just one win in their previous ten league outings although one of their three wins away from home had come rather disconcertingly at promotion-chasing Burnley.

But that was way back in October and any fears that Lions fans may have had about Scunny springing another shock appeared to be allayed when Cahill grabbed his third goal in one and a half matches to give Millwall a 1-0 half time lead.

They had gone into the match in third place, just four points behind leaders Bristol Rovers and three adrift of Preston. The main fly in the ointment was that Millwall had played one game more than the leaders and two more than North End.

As news filtered through of half time scores elsewhere, Bristol Rovers were retaining their advantage at the top with a 1-0 lead at the break against Wycombe. More interestingly, Preston were trailing 0-1 at home to Colchester meaning that only goal difference now separated Millwall from an automatic promotion place. That goal difference was a whopping eight goals, but surely now, with their foot firmly on Scunthorpe's neck, was the time to put on a repeat performance of the previous game's four-goal display and really start to put the pressure on.

Two Scunthorpe goals in ten minutes midway through the second half put Millwall's promotion aspirations well and truly back into perspective. Preston had indeed gone on to lose - 2-3 at home to Colchester, but Bristol Rovers continued to defy those so-called experts who were dismissing them as a pacemaker ready to fall by the promotion wayside, holding on to a 1-0 win over Wycombe courtesy of a Nathan Ellington goal.

There was some dismay at how Ellington had been able to escape Millwall's clutches. Starting at Walton and Hersham - a club that Millwall chairman Theo Paphitis had been involved with when the player was spotted, he had gone on to become one of the lower divisions' most prolific strikers. Of course, these things happen all the time in football and Paphitis couldn't be held responsible for The Lions missing that particular goalscoring sensation. Although he was being blamed for Millwall not signing another.

Legendary striker Ian Wright had recently joined promotion rivals Burnley, but shortly after making the move to Turf Moor, the ex Palace and Arsenal hitman went public with details of how he was close to joining his boyhood local side Millwall, only for the deal to be scuppered by chairman Theo Paphitis. The livewire Lions' chairman needed no prompting to put the record straight and reinforce his increasing disdain for the game's agents and their behaviour in such transfers:

"I think Ian is a top bloke and very passionate about his football. But in this instance he appears to have been fed a load of garbage by his agent which apparently he has cared to repeat in a newspaper. The truth is that we were keen to get Ian here. He's an infectious character who might have given the club a lift at this stage of the season. Within about 30 seconds of originally speaking to Ian on the subject, I rang his agent and had a long conver-

sation with two people at the agency who then promised to ring me back. Eventually they did get back to me at about 10.30pm on the Sunday night with some outrageous demands when they had clearly already done a deal with Burnley. I have no problem with Ian, but I think he needs to check with his agents that they are really giving him the full story. Initially I had hoped that we could have come to some sort of arrangement with Ian, although not for the sort of figures I was quoted on the Sunday night. But one sticking point certainly might have been the fact that I could not guarantee him a place in the side every week. I told him that the decision as to who plays was down to Rhino and Macca, and that we already have some very good strikers at the club. The fact that we have scored nine goals and won three games since these discussions took place would appear to bear that out, even with Neil Harris on the sidelines. Of course we would have liked to add Ian to the equation, but we certainly couldn't have told him that he would be in the side every week no matter what. On the subject of agents, I'm very concerned about this aspect of the game. Don't get me wrong, there are some very good ones around, but there are also some very bad ones and what concerns me most at the moment is those that hang around school gates promising untold riches to 14-year-olds. I will be bringing this whole matter up at the next Chairmen's conference in June, because I think that we need to set a lower age limit for agents' involvement in order to protect young players. The PFA, the strongest union in Europe, have trained staff who can look after the interests of these youngsters, and who have their best interests at heart. This is not always the case with agents, who more often than not are just out to see what they can make for themselves."

Millwall fans may have been kicking themselves at the fact that they had seemingly missed out on one of the game's greatest ever strikers who, despite coming to the end of his career would surely find goals easy to come by at this level. But, as Theo rightly pointed out, Millwall did already have an abundance of striking talent both old and new that should have been enough to get the goals required to earn promotion. Whether Burnley's acquisition of Wright would prove to be the difference would soon be revealed.

In the shock aftermath of the Scunthorpe defeat, much blame was aimed at stand-in defender Dave Tuttle who was deputising for the absent Scott Fitzgerald. This seemed a little unfair given that Tuttle had put in a solid performance in the 4-1 against Bristol City three days earlier but all football fans love a scapegoat and the facts were Millwall had, as a team, once gain worked themselves into an excellent position to make progress at the top of the table, only to let it slip through their fingers.

Fortunately, retribution was swift as Cahill made it a remarkable five goals in three matches in an impressive first half display in the 2-0 win at Luton but frustration loomed once more as the following weekend it took a Harris penalty on the stroke of half time to cancel out an earlier Blackpool goal and with the struggling Seasiders holding on for dear life in the second period Millwall were once again forced to settle for a home draw - and fail to beat a side in the bottom places.

On the same day, Ian Wright scored his second goal since signing for Burnley - after getting his first in the midweek draw with Gillingham and his side, which Millwall had managed to keep at arms length because of their somewhat shot-shy record, were now starting to score goals - and make up ground on The Lions.

Yet another 1-1 draw - this time away to Wrexham saw The Lions drop to fourth place once more, and it was only thanks to another late Michael Gilkes goal that the trip to north Wales wasn't completely pointless. It wasn't the best preparation for the visit of table-topping Bristol Rovers, a side who Millwall had struggled badly against in recent years. Now, at the end of March, The Lions were faced with the real prospect of clinging on to a play-off spot when, just a month earlier, top place was within reach.

Millwall had managed just four victories over Rovers in 26 meetings - spanning all the way back to 1976 which included a woeful record of seven defeats in the eight matches the two sides played between 1991 and 1997.

It was Bristol Rovers who provided the ignominious 0-3 reverse on the historic final match at the old Den back in amongst that run in 1993.

Now Millwall needed to turn those stats on their head if they were to revive any hopes they had of a top two place - with trips to Preston and Burnley looming on the horizon.

Bristol Rovers arrived at The Den having been displaced at the top of the able by in-form Preston who had hit top spot thanks to a three match wining streak. Rovers' form was by no means shabby but the two wins in five March matches was to prove the start of their season's decline. For once, Millwall were to play a team at just the right time.

Goals from Harris, Sadlier and Ifill blew Rovers away and equalled The Lions' biggest post-war victory over The Pirates who would go on to win just one more match for the rest of the season. They had spent all but the first three weeks of the campaign inside the top six but would drop outside the play-off zone on the final day. The only problem was, even with Bristol Rovers out of the top two place, others were approaching fast.

Sadly, the glorious result had been achieved against another backdrop of controversy. Millwall had always enjoyed a good relationship with its local newspaper *The South London Press*, but a story that had appeared in the paper following The Lions' previous home match with Blackpool had thrown that relationship into turmoil.

Once again, chairman Theo Paphitis was quick to address the situation and his increasingly eloquent and fierce defence of his football club was quickly becoming an invaluable piece of the club's armour against the injustices of the media.

The issue surrounded a planned visit of Kosovan asylum seekers to Millwall's match with Blackpool - which was the club's annual anti-racism focus match. Following on from reports in the paper about crowd violence at London Bridge station between rival fans after the home match with Bristol City, Paphitis contact the paper to point out numerous inaccuracies in the story which amounted to there actually being no incidents at all - which was backed up by the Football Liaison Officer present at the time.

A furious Paphitis penned the following letter to the Chief Executive of Trinity Newspapers, of which the South London Press was then a part of:

Dear Mr Graffe,

Re: Millwall Football Club and the South London Press.

You may by now be aware that relationships between Millwall Football Club and the South London Press have become seriously strained over the past fortnight, to the point where it could have a lasting, damaging effect. We are concerned that this turn of events has been allowed to occur, since for the most part, we have enjoyed an harmonious and cordial relationship with the paper for the past several years. From our perspective, the background to our dispute with the SLP, and in particular with the Editor, Ms. Hannah Walker, surrounds examples of grossly irresponsible journalism which have had a damaging effect on the club and the community. I had cause to take issue with Ms Walker barely a fortnight ago, after she ran a story about violence involving Millwall and Bristol City fans at London Bridge station which was riddled with factual inaccuracies, to the extent that no such violence occurred. The Football Liaison Officer who was present with the fans at London Bridge Station at the time, dismissed the account as 'Rubbish.' Having discussed this matter with Ms Walker, and reached what I had hoped, was some understanding of how such reporting can have a very negative effect in terms of people's perception of Millwall Football Club, I have been incredulous at the way in which her paper has reported the story surrounding a proposed visit to The Den of a small group of Kosovan Asylum seekers. In the SLP dated 10th March 2000, a story entitled 'Millwall meet their new fans' appeared outlining the initiative by Southwark Police (erroneously attributed to Southwark Council) to bring the group to our Anti-Racism Focus Match against Blackpool on March 18th. The journalist in question could not resist the temptation to 'sensationalise' with the following observation; "But since they started moving into the hotel in September 1997, there have been increased reports of shoplifting and harassment of female shoppers and staff at the nearby shopping centre. In December, a centre security guard was stabbed and last month a black member of the hotel staff was attacked by a Kosovan gang." Once the above had been linked unnecessarily to the story since it was not new, the prospect of the visit going ahead in a positive and peaceful manner was condemned to failure. Ms Walker expressed astonishment that the tabloids had a field day. The best I can attribute to her is naïvety in the extreme. It must have been clear to her that there has been a negative campaign in the popular press surrounding Kosovan Asylum Seekers, and that the nature of her paper's reporting of this story would be grist to the mill. The Sun's approach certainly came as no surprise to me. Unsurprisingly, the decision was taken by Southwark Police, in consultation with ourselves, that the Kosovan visit could not take place for fear that individuals or groups might use it as an opportunity to make political capital out of the situation. They were aware, as we were, not only of the security implications, but of the disruptive effect that agents provocateurs could have had on a well planned and positive event, and that some 1600 children and Special Needs groups would be present on the day. The SLP's reporting of the cancellation of the visit (14th March 2000) contained the following untruths: 1) "Southwark cops cancelled their plans to take a coach load of Kosovar nationals to the game against Blackpool for fear of racial violence erupting on the terraces."

The implication here is that Millwall fans, inside the ground, who were racially motivated, would resort to violence as a result of the Kosovan presence. How much more damaging can you get to the image of Millwall than this, since neither the club, nor Lewisham police who are responsible for policing games here, had any such concerns.

2) "But the move prompted a fierce backlash from racists who phoned the club."

Not true, and again incredibly emotive and damaging by implication.

3) The quote from Inspector Steve Burgess, as set out in a Press Release from the Metropolitan Police on 13th March 2000 was clear:

"However, it has been decided to postpone the visit to The Den. Both Southwark and Lewisham Councils have invited a number of school groups, including those with Special Needs to the game. Their safety and enjoyment of the occasion, in addition to that of other supporters, cannot

be allowed to be compromised by those who might seek to make political capital out of the situation." By missing out the sentence referring to the school groups and those with Special Needs; the whole sense of the piece is changed, inferring that the safety and enjoyment only of the Kosovans was paramount, and by implication the 'racist' slant is heightened. The fact that this story was given the highest profile, on the front page with its sensational angle was again guaranteed to fuel the national media. No surprise then that the Telegraph led with a story entitled, Millwall bite the hand of friendship on the very day that we had gone out of our way to extend it. Unfortunately, Ms Walker seems to be totally oblivious to the effect that words can have on other people, and of her responsibility as the editor of a newspaper. My subsequent discussions with her, which I must say were reluctant on my part, appear to have widened the gap between us. Veiled threats about the damage that lack of coverage in her paper might have on us, and questioning of our commitment to outlawing racism are hardly designed to ease the tension.

Millwall is centred in a multi-racial community, and our initiatives towards combating racism within football and society in general are well known. March 18th 2000 was our third Annual Anti-Racism Focus Day, not something we had dreamed up on the spur of the moment. In the face of this fact, the South London Press reports seem more likely to incite racial tension than help to allay such fears. I know Dr Les Back, Chair of the South London Kick-It Out campaign has expressed such a view to Ms Walker in writing, whilst Asquith Gibbes, Chair of Millwall's Anti-Racism Committee, is also gravely concerned at the fall out from these articles, as indeed are members of both Lewisham and Southwark Councils, with whom we have been working closely for some years on these issues. The bottom line is that it is the responsibility of Ms Walker to report the news, not to create it. My deep suspicion is that she saw the opportunity to attract attention from the big players in her field and went for it, irrespective of the consequences. The South London Press lit the touch paper and waited for the conflagration. In so doing she has betrayed our trust in her paper and, as a result, it is difficult at this juncture to see a resolution to the breakdown in our relationship.

Yours sincerely

Theo Paphitis

The new SLP editor Hannah Walker must have been staggered at this response, almost certainly thinking the club would simply lie down and take such scandalous untruths and sensationalism. She would remain in the position for almost 18 years, but never dared to cross the club again, no doubt learning never to mess with Millwall.

Daydreams & Nightmares - Millwall FC in the 2000s - Part 1

3. The old enemy returns

April 2000...
4 April – Charlie Kray, one of the infamous Kray brothers, dies in a hospital on the Isle of Wight after suffering a heart attack in Parkhurst Prison at age 73; 14 April – Kenneth Noye, the so-called "M25 killer", is sentenced to life imprisonment...

April began with what was starting to be a season-defining result for Millwall: A 1-1 draw away to a Notts County side that had the merest sniff of a final play-off place. What was encouraging was that Neil Harris had seemingly rediscovered his goalscoring touch after absence through injury and suspension and had given The Lions a half time lead, which was cancelled out on the hour mark by County's Darby.

At least the home form had returned and Bury were quickly despatched with goals from Moody, Harris and young defender Dolan in the first half giving The Lions another morale-boosting 3-0 win. This was followed up by Neil Harris' first league hat-trick for the club as Millwall completed the double over Brentford with a 3-1 win at Griffin Park. It was perfect preparation for the next seven days which could see The Lions clinch an automatic promotion place with games at fifth-placed Burnley, sixth-placed Gillingham and top-of-the-table Preston. Although maximum points from those games was a big ask, especially with Burnley and Preston being two of Millwall's less happy hunting grounds, Lions fans had to hope that this little bit of momentum they had found could be carried into them - and what better motivation than to be able to go into the final match of the season at home to Oxford on 87 points where a win would take them to 90 and almost guaranteed automatic promotion.

The week leading up to the Easter Saturday trip to Burnley's Turf Moor was a torturous one for Millwall fans who will have been pouring over the league table and trying to work out if they could perhaps afford to grab a draw from either of the tricky trips to Lancashire, and perhaps nick a win at the other and rely on ending the season at home with two straight wins. That would be 88 points - would it be enough for second place?

Burnley were just two points behind The Lions with a much easier run-in. A draw there might not been enough, defeat was unthinkable. Burnley's build-up to the match had been a three game winning run, brought to an abrupt halt with a stinging 0-3 home reverse to Gillingham. Whether they were ripe for Millwall to pick their pocket, or would bounce back was another conundrum to throw into the prematch mix.

By the time Burnley's Paul Cook slotted home Burnley's fourth goal in just the 52nd minute of the match, all automatic promotion permutations had become irrelevant. Stan Ternant's side had blown Millwall away with goals at the beginning, middle and end of the first half sending a shell-shocked Lions into the half time break 0-3 behind. A Neil Harris consolation on the hour wasn't enough to prevent a large portion of the travelling Millwall fans from making their way out of the stadium, unable to bear the torture any longer.

But they were quickly returning when Harris netted again with almost fifteen minutes left and a Cahill goal on 87 minutes had them dreaming of an unlikely, but very useful point. Burnley, to use Ternant's words after the match, were defending from under their own crossbar, but defend they did and the match finished 3-4.

The Clarets had spent the last five months sitting in fifth place, waiting to pounce, and now they had. They were, it seemed, the horse making the late run for the finishing post and now, with them leap-frogging Millwall, there was nothing The Lions could do to catch them, except win all of their remaining three matches and hope they slipped up.

If nerves were jangling going into the match at Burnley, they were positively frazzled 48 hours later when Gillingham visited The Den. Millwall had now slipped to fifth with Gillingham breathing down their necks, just three points behind. Another defeat would see another contender overtake them and leave The Lions suddenly clinging to a last play-off spot instead of pushing for the top two.

Conversely, that automatic promotion place was still not out of reach, currently occupied by Wigan, just three points ahead of Millwall. Top spot was gone. Preston were flying with an eight point lead, the title was theirs in all but name. Wigan's run-in, like Burnley's, was quite favourable though. Bristol Rovers were well and truly on the decline, a 2-0 win over bitter rivals City on Easter Saturday giving them brief hope of a final push but they looked like a team who had run out of steam and were happy to settle for a play-off place.

The problem with that was, for both Millwall and Bristol Rovers, Stoke had suddenly clicked into gear too. For almost the entire season they had been hovering around seventh or eight place and had now won three in a row to put themselves just two points outside a play-off berth

- and just five behind The Lions. Millwall had to go for Gillingham from the first whistle and make sure they got back to winning ways.

An incredible sell-out crowd of just under 18,000, with 3,500 packing the away end, turned out on an idyllic sunny Easter Monday for one of the biggest matches for either club in many a year. The pre-match atmosphere was an understandable mix of excitement, tension and typical Millwall ferocity and all of these ingredients exploded in the seventh minute.

After withstanding some Gillingham pressure in the first five minutes, Tony Warner gathered a Gills cross and threw the ball out to the waiting Paul Ifill on the right hand side. He quickly made inroads into the Gillingham half and picked out Lucas Neill on the opposite side, just on the corner of the 18 yard box. Neill jinked inside and found Paul Moody on the opposite corner who stroked home a superbly placed shot into the top corner of the net to send Millwall's biggest ever league crowd at the New Den totally berserk.

Straight from the restart Gillingham lost possession and Millwall again broke down the right hand side. Matt Lawrence found Harris who cut the ball back for Ifill to finish with equal aplomb. Millwall were in total control of the most crucial match of their season.

Had this been a Bristol City, Bristol Rovers or Bury - which is what Millwall fans were now expecting, the floodgates would have opened. But this Gillingham side were no mugs and just four minutes later Gooden struck back for the Kent side with a long range effort that went in off Warner's left post.

Suddenly the entire complexion of the game changed and Gillingham poured forward. Then just as Millwall fans felt they had survived until half time and a chance to galvanise for the second half to protect the three points, Gillingham midfielder Andy Hessenthaler was allowed to run unchallenged down the left flank, cut inside the area and unleash an unstoppable shot to level the match at 2-2.

The second period was no less frantic and it looked as if Moody would restore the lead when he met an Ifill cross form the right perfectly on the edge of the six yard box, but just as the home fans prepared to erupt once more, Gills' stopper Bartram pulled off an incredible save to deny the veteran frontman.

Moments later there was a goal for Millwall fans to celebrate when Cahill rose to head home what was becoming a trademark goal of his. He beat Bartram to the aerial ball and as it dropped on the line it was bundled into the net by a Gills defender trying to clear. The joy was short-lived however, referee Paul Rejer deeming Cahill had used an arm to gain an unfair aerial advantage over Bartram, and the match appeared to be fizzling out to a draw.

There was still time for some drama at the other end however when Gillingham's substitute striker Carl Asaba turned neatly on the edge of the area and smashed his shot against the bar with Warner well beaten. The rebound was almost put over the line by an onrushing Gooden, but Millwall were able to clear the danger.

The celebrations in the away end that greeted the final whistle told its own story as home fans trudged away wondering how they hadn't managed to win the match.

Now on just 79 points with a trip to newly-crowned champions Preston to come, a maximum possible tally of 85 would almost certainly not be enough for a top two spot - especially with Burnley winning to stretch their lead over The Lions to four points.

There was a horrifying feeling of deja vu seven days later when Millwall's beleaguered players left the Deepdale pitch for the tunnel at half time. In a carnival atmosphere that Millwall had hoped was awaiting them the following weekend at The Den, Preston had celebrated winning the title in style by racing into a 3-0 half time lead.

The first came in the opening minute of the game, by the eighth minute it was 2-0 and all over. The third came on the brink of half time and Millwall were now suffering their worst run of form since the opening weeks of the season.

Bizarrely, as at Turf Moor seven days later, Millwall staged what would again prove to be a fruitless second half comeback. In fact they gave themselves much more of a chance to grab a completely unlikely victory with goals from Ifill and Neill putting them within one goal of their hosts just eight minutes into the second half. But it was to prove another season-defining result that would deprive them of a top two place. Slow starts - both in terms of the season as a whole and crucial matches - denied Millwall the vital points they required for an automatic promotion place.

However it was suddenly much worse than that. Far from missing out on automatic promotion, Millwall's winless week had seen them drop out of the top six altogether for the first time since November 1999. Just seven days ago, Lions fans were hopeful of a runners-up spot being clinched in the final match of the season at home to Oxford.

Now they needed others to slip up just to earn a place in the play-offs!

Nationwide League Division 2 - May 6th 2000							
	P	W	D	L	F	A	PTS
1. Preston (C)	45	27	11	7	72	37	92
2. Gillingham	45	25	10	10	79	47	85
3. Burnley	45	24	13	8	67	46	85
4. Wigan	45	22	16	7	70	36	82
5. Stoke	45	23	13	9	68	41	82
6. Bristol Rovers	45	23	11	11	69	44	80
7. Millwall	**45**	**22**	**13**	**10**	**75**	**50**	**79**

The table, as is always the case, never lies when the final reckoning is made at the end of the season. However unlikely it was for Millwall to have won those three matches in that crucial week, maximum points from them would have indeed seen them needing just to beat Oxford on the final day to guarantee runners up spot behind Preston.

The table also showed both Millwall's strengths over the other promotion-chasing clubs - and its key weakness. The Lions had scored more than any of the top six above them, but also conceded more. That said, there was very little to separate the clubs in second to seventh place in what had been another closely fought Division Two campaign.

The bitterest pill for Millwall fans as they assembled for the last time in the league at The Den was that, had they managed to adhere to the age old promotion formula of winning at home and drawing away in those fateful three matches where they managed just a single point, the permutations for that final match would have been for an automatic promotion place.

As it was, here were the scenarios as The Lions kicked off against Oxford:

Obviously Millwall had to do their bit and win. If they did, and Bristol Rovers failed to win at Cardiff, Millwall would clinch a play-off spot.

A Millwall draw might still be enough, if Rovers were to lose at Cardiff, The Lions' slightly superior goal difference would be enough for them to pip Ian Holloway's side by the slimmest of margins.

Fifth place was even possible with a Millwall win and slip-ups for both Rovers and Stoke.

A typically tense affair in front of a slightly disappointing crowd of 13,000 was settled with a seventh-minute Neil Harris goal. With both Stoke and Bristol Rovers losing, Millwall had clinched fifth place. Gillingham agonisingly missed out on automatic promotion with defeat at Wrexham, which left the path clear for Stan Ternent's Burnley to nick the second and final automatic promotion place with a 2-1 win at Scunthorpe.

It was their fourth win in a row - something that Millwall needed to achieve when they had travelled to Turf Moor just two weeks earlier - and it was only the second time Burnley had made it into the top two places all season. The previous time being a one week spell back at the start of the season. Bristol Rovers' fall from grace had been quite spectacular, looking certainties for the title at one stage but missing out altogether on the final day - the first time they had been outside the top six since August, proving how cruel and unforgiving football can be.

Wigan's fade was also a surprise. They looked dominant at various stages of the season but ended it with a whimper with just one win in their last six matches.

All the talk now was of momentum going into the play-offs where Stoke were looking good having clinched their sixth place with a run of six wins on the spin - a record only spoiled by that final day loss. They would play Gillingham.

There's never really a team you'd rather face in the play-offs. Results between teams in the league become irrelevant - as Millwall found out in their previous two play-off disasters against Brighton and Derby who they had the better of during the season but were well beaten by in the two-leg lottery.

Both Gillingham and Stoke would have proved tough opponents so they might have been happy not to face them, but those final day results had meant that they would face a team quickly becoming something of an unlikely rival: Wigan.

Millwall had faced The Latics in the previous season's Auto Windscreens Shield final confident they could be victorious at Wembley against a team they had got the better of over two league games. The lost 0-1. Now, after two draws in the league, there was no barometer for how these two games would go, the first being at The Den. Both sides went into the matches on a low, having had aspirations of a top two place until the penultimate match of the regular season, but both knew the simple formula for winning promotion now was: draw away, win at home, then you're just one win away from glory.

Another packed Den saw Millwall throw everything at Wigan, but another of those tell-tale stats in that final league table went against The Lions. Wigan had the most miserly defence and avoiding defeat away from home had been the linchpin of their success. They had suffered defeat just twice on the road, although the 13 draws they took back home may have been instrumental in them not making the top two.

At home they were beatable, losing five and Millwall had come close to taking all three points with a depleted lineup when they had drawn 1-1 there. But 15 wins - one more than even Millwall's impressive home form could manage - meant that Wigan were hot favourites to seal the tie when the final whistle blew at a goalless Den.

There was a certain inevitability about the routine way Wigan took the lead and sat back on it in the second leg. Millwall's efforts were brave, but ultimately too tame to break a stubborn Wigan defence down and The Lions' promotion dream once again died in the play-offs, this time without even a goal to cheer or bring hope.

Keith Stevens and Alan McLeary now had the tough task of picking their players up and strengthening the squad to try and make another push next season.

NATIONWIDE LEAGUE DIVISION TWO
FINAL TABLE 1999/2000

1	**Preston North End**	46	28	11	7	74	37	+37	95
2	**Burnley**	46	25	13	8	69	47	+22	88
3	**Gillingham**	46	25	10	11	79	48	+31	85
4	Wigan Athletic	46	22	17	7	72	38	+34	83
5	**MILLWALL**	46	23	13	10	76	50	+26	82
6	Stoke City	46	23	13	10	68	42	+26	82
7	Bristol Rovers	46	23	11	12	69	45	+24	80
8	Notts County	46	18	11	17	61	55	+6	65
9	Bristol City	46	15	19	12	59	57	+2	64
10	Reading	46	16	14	16	57	63	−6	62
11	Wrexham	46	17	11	18	52	61	−9	62
12	Wycombe Wanderers	46	16	13	17	56	53	+3	61
13	Luton Town	46	17	10	19	61	65	−4	61
14	Oldham Athletic	46	16	12	18	50	55	−5	60
15	Bury	46	13	18	15	61	64	−3	57
16	Bournemouth	46	16	9	21	59	62	−3	57
17	Brentford	46	13	13	20	47	61	−14	52
18	Colchester United	46	14	10	22	59	82	−23	52
19	Cambridge United	46	12	12	22	64	65	−1	48
20	Oxford United	46	12	9	25	43	73	−30	45
21	**Cardiff City**	46	9	17	20	45	67	−22	44
22	**Blackpool**	46	8	17	21	49	77	−28	41
23	**Scunthorpe United**	46	9	12	25	40	74	−34	39
24	**Chesterfield**	46	7	15	24	34	63	−29	36

cheer up ...

00/01

Daydreams & Nightmares - Millwall FC in the 2000s - Part 1

4. Tough Love

July 2000
14 July – Reality television game show Big Brother first airs in the UK; 20 July – Production of the Ford Escort, one of Britain's most successful and iconic motoring nameplates, finishes after 32 years; Rioting breaks out in Brixton following the fatal shooting of Derek Bennett, a 29-year-old black man, by armed police in the area. 27 people are arrested and three police officers are injured...

Never a club to indulge in self pity, Millwall were quick to put the disappointment of missing out in the play-offs yet again behind them. In fact, going into the new season, Wigan were almost certainly feeling more downbeat than The Lions. The Lancashire big spenders had been installed as firm favourites to win the Wembley play-off final against a Gillingham side who had come from mid-table to land a late shot at an automatic promotion place and then edge past Stoke in their semi-final. Having lost the first leg in The Potteries 2-3, The Gills eased to the final with a 3-0 second leg win but were not fancied to oust The Latics in the final. But they disproved the doubters with another free-scoring display in a thrilling final that saw Wigan's watertight defence that had kept

Millwall at bay in the semi-final leak three times. The Gills took a first half lead but were pegged back in the second half and when Wigan scored an extra time penalty they appeared to be heading for promotion, only for Gillingham to strike twice in the final six minutes to win the match 3-2.

New opponents for Millwall would be Walsall, Swindon and Port Vale coming down from Division One, and Swansea, Rotherham, Northampton and Peterborough coming up from the Third Division. Only Wigan and Stoke were considered any threat to Millwall's early installation as one of the Division Two title favourites, but as we know, that is something that can often work against you.

Pre-season had been impressive with the pick of the wins being a 6-0 drubbing of Crystal Palace. There were no new arrivals - something which raised an eyebrow or two amongst fans that assembled for the season opener against Reading at The Den, but management duo Stevens and McLeary felt the side that had come so close the previous season clearly deserved a chance to show it could push on in what was felt to be a slightly weaker division this time around. There was a major departure however, striker Paul Shaw leaving for newly-promoted Gillingham for a deal worth up to £500,000. Up front was felt to be Millwall's stronger area and, injury and suspensions permitting, it was felt the goals from Harris, Sadlier and Moody would be enough.

Rhino and Macca's judgement appeared well-placed as Millwall eased to a solid-looking 2-0 opening day win against Alan Pardew's Royals thanks to two goals from Tim Cahill five minutes into each period.

Cahill's goals were further evidence of The Lions' strike power - and with Paul Ifill also regularly weighing in with a few, the only thing required to turn last season's play-off failure into automatic promotion was a solid defence and the rub of the green with injuries. Goals were flowing in the first away match when Moody gave The Lions a fourteenth-minute lead at Notts County and despite being pegged back on the half hour, Reid and Harris strikes sent Millwall in comfortable at the break 3-1 ahead.

But the old defensive frailties resurfaced in the second half as goals from Ramage and Stallard squared the match at 3-3 with fifteen minutes left. Fortunately a last-minute Bircham strike from outside the area in front of Millwall's jubilant travelling fans was enough to rescue all three points and settle a seven-goal humdinger. With the next three league matches all at home, The Lions had a chance to open up an early lead at the top of the table and send out a message to the rest.

With a 2-1 League Cup first leg win at Brighton also under their belts, Millwall looked to be starting the season in fine style when an eleventh-minute Neil Harris goal gave them a 1-0 half time lead in the next league match at home to Wycombe Wanderers. But in an explicable 20 second half minutes, Millwall's defence once again went missing as goals from Baird and Bullman turned the match on its head and gave The Lions their first home reverse of the season in just the second match.

The next match at The Den wasn't much better, Brighton holding Millwall to a 1-1 draw which saw The Lions edge through to round two 3-2 on aggregate, and it was to get worse. Whilst Harris was on target again to help his side return to winning ways with a last-minute midweek winner against Swansea, the boos from the sparsely-populated Den attendance of barely 7,000 following Northampton's 1-0 victory three days later were punctuated, for the first time, with calls for the management duo of Stevens and McLeary to be sacked.

Even by Millwall's standards, this sudden change in

fortunes and fan sentiment was a shock and it was quickly becoming clear that Stevens and McLeary had gone from being lauded as the club's saviours to being on borrowed time as they prepared to travel to Brentford and get the promotion charge back on track.

The atmosphere in the visitors' section of Brentford's tight little Griffin Park ground was tense from the first whistle, made all the more incendiary by its close proximity to the pitch.

When Andy Scott gave the home side a 51st-minute lead the mood turned palpably toxic. Even Neil Harris' equaliser ten minutes from time couldn't appease Millwall's furious followers who had now seen their team capitulate in spectacular fashion over the course of the last four games.

With Millwall lying in 13th place in the table and, just six games in, already losing as many home matches as they had throughout the whole of last season, the unerring silence following the draw at Brentford was eventually broken the following day when it was announced that Millwall had parted company with management duo Keith Stevens and Alan McLeary.

When he had appointed the pair, Chairman Theo Paphitis had raised a few eyebrows by admitting that, during the meeting, he told them: *"You do realise by making you managers, one day I'm going to have to sack two Millwall legends?"*

One thing Theo had proved in his relatively short tenure at Millwall though was that he was fully aware that there was no room for sentiment in football - just as there wasn't in any of his business dealings. He knew that, one day, the time would come when Rhino and Macca had taken the club as far as they could.

Fans must also have realised that deep down, and in many ways understood Theo's comments. However, the pace at which Stevens and McLeary had developed the club must have had most supporters assuming that day might come *after* promotion had been won to a higher level rather than so early before. In some ways, the pair had almost been victims of their own success. The rapid progress they had made since taking over the reigns from Billy Bonds a little over two years earlier was nothing short of miraculous. Whilst it could be pointed out that they did inherit the nucleus of the useful squad they handed over, as a club Millwall was still very rudderless and distant from the fans until they made their mark.

To take Millwall from there to Wembley and within a couple of wins of promotion in the brief time it took meant the bar had been set very high and whilst glitches are part and parcel at all football clubs that are headed in the right direction, there was increasing evidence during those final games of Stevens and McLeary's tenure that the momentum had lost power and they had perhaps started to struggle keeping control of that rudder.

Such was Paphitis' candour - so rare for football chairmen who revel in such clichés as "mutual agreements" and "taken the club as far as they could" - the decision could almost be seen as an act of tough love, such was his acknowledgement of the respect Millwall fans had for Stevens and McLeary. Had he allowed them to fail and sack them after not delivering promotion at a time when success was expected possibly more than any time in the club's history, their legacy would have been one of failure. A harsh one for two such decorated Lions stalwarts.

As it stood, they were able to walk away leaving the history books to show that they took over a Millwall team with an identity crisis and a new chairman finding his way around the club, and indelibly re-stamped the club with its unmistakable pride, leaving Paphitis in no doubt exactly what the fans expected.

They may not have been able to get Millwall back up, but they certainly got the fans their Millwall back.

While Paphitis began, what would have seemed a few weeks earlier, a highly unlikely search for a new manager, Ray Harford and Steve Gritt were put in temporary charge of team affairs for the next match - the League Cup second round first leg tie at home to Premier League Ipswich Town.

One of the first pieces of business the new temporary management team oversaw was the loan signing of striker Sam Parkin from Chelsea, mindful that The Lions had once again inexplicably dried up in the goals department.

A morale-boosting 2-0 win over top flight Ipswich set the team up nicely for the visit of Oxford and, whilst the programme notes from Theo Paphitis explained that the search for a new manager was still much a work in progress, those who caught sight of ex Reading, Leicester and Wolves manager Mark McGhee in The Den's West Stand were twigging that progress had quickly come to what many fans felt was a highly unsatisfactory conclusion.

McGhee must have been impressed with what he was allegedly about to inherit as Millwall found their goalscoring mojo once more in a 5-0 demolition of Oxford.

Parkin made a dream start to his Lions career smashing the first home after just two minutes and Neil Harris capitalised on a goalkeeping howler to make it two after half an hour before grabbing his second just before the break. The impressive Parkin added another and Harris completed his second hat-trick for the club to seal a real tonic of a victory after a harrowing few weeks for club and fans.

Harford and Gritt remained in charge for the League Cup exit away to Ipswich - where Millwall ended the match with nine men after seeing their 2-0 first leg advantage erased with just two minutes left, eventually losing 0-5 on the night after extra time and 2-5 on aggregate. With cup distractions out of the way, Mark McGhee was officially unveiled as Millwall's new manager in time for the league visit to Peterborough. The build-up to the trip to London Road was punctuated by a less than welcoming response from Millwall fans at the official unveiling of McGhee as the club's 31st managerial appointment.

McGhee had shot to prominence after hanging up his prolific goalscoring boots and guiding Reading to the Division Two title in 1994. He had been recommended for the post by none other than Sir Alex Ferguson who had made him his first major signing after taking over the reigns at Aberdeen.

After Reading continued their trajectory during the following season he agreed a long term deal with The Royals who recognised his value and the potential for him to take them into The Premier League for the first time. With Reading in second place going into the end of 1994 McGhee stunned fans by accepting the position at top flight strugglers Leicester.

He was unable to stop them from dropping down into Division One where Reading remained after losing the play-off final to Bolton.

After spending the summer assembling a squad to make an immediate return, McGhee's Leicester looked good for promotion back to The Premier League - only for him to stun fans once more by moving to Wolves just 12 months after he had joined.

Taking over from Graham Taylor, McGhee was unable to reignite the expected promotion charge and the club ended the season escaping relegation by just three points, while the Leicester side he built won promotion via the play-offs.

Better followed next season but the pressure on him to

deliver increased when, after a summer of huge spending, what at one point looked a certain second place automatic promotion place ended in play-off semi-final defeat and a stinging rebuke from Wolves owner Jack Hayward who tightened the transfer budget purse strings and dismissed son Jonathan who was the chairman that had appointed McGhee.

After missing out on the play-offs the following season and a run of just two wins in twelve at the start of the 1998/99 campaign, McGhee was relieved of his duties and, in the light of the reputation that his ship-jumping at both Reading and Leicester had earned him, suddenly found himself in the managerial wilderness.

To Millwall fans, this was not the sort of CV befitting a manager charged with taking over from two of the most loyal servants the club had ever produced.

Internet discussion forums were quickly gaining on the pub as the main venue of footballing debate by now and Millwall had one of the first ones to appear on the world wide web.

House of Fun had been launched by IT engineer and Kingston University research, postgraduate and undergraduate student and Lions fan Paul Neve in 1996.

It was a time when just connecting to the Internet required a computer science degree and anyone who felt the need to set themselves up with an email account will have spent months staring at an empty inbox after disabling their home phone in order to connect to the noisy, clunky, painfully slow new technological gimmick.

The site had originally been called "You'll Never Make The Station", a tongue-in-cheek title based on the terrace chant that was commonplace during the 70s when Millwall's hooligan reputation really started to build in the aftermath of the infamous Panorama documentary. The irony being that its creator and initial handful of members couldn't have been further from the media perception of "A Millwall Fan".

Neve curated a ground breaking online community that was a perfect blend of his technical skill, football knowledge and passion for the club.

It grew as quickly as Internet take-up accelerated at the end of the century and Neve opted for the slightly more palatable moniker of House of Fun (a nod to the Madness hit chorus' second line: "Welcome to The Lions Den".

By 2000, HoF as it became affectionately known, had hundreds of members who spent hours every day debating the various goings on at the club under mysterious pseudonyms such as Albert, TAMP, or Tea and in September 2000 it was experiencing a bandwidth-busting surge of activity as keyboards smoked with posts raging at the new appointment in levels of hysteria that only the Internet could entertain.

The media were quickly cottoning on to this new insight into football fans' opinion and, never ones to ignore an easy way to create copy, were to fall into a brilliantly set trap by Neve, decades ahead of Wagatha Christie.

He was suspicious that some contentious topics discussed on the forum seemed to be appearing in the news in brief columns of the red tops. The fact that the main forum was called "Controversial Corner" must have been like catnip for lazy journos. This theory was boosted by the fact that the site's newby lurker count peaked at the same time. A newby being a new member signing up and a lurker being someone who is viewing the messageboard but not taking part in any discussions.

Such was Neve's attention to detail and technical knowledge, he was able to quickly avail himself of this information that any muck-mongering hack would have been blissfully unaware of, and so, like any self-respecting scientist, hatched an experiment that was to yield quite delicious results, way beyond what he could have imagined.

Airline, a fly-on-the-wall television documentary about the budget airline Easyjet was huge at the time, making its CEO Stelios a household name. Millwall chairman Theo Paphitis had, with Paul Neve's knowledge and blessing, made a temporary appearance on HoF's Controversial Corner to address fans' concerns about recent events at the club, something which, understandably made its way into the inner reaches of the sporting editions if for nothing else than novelty value. "Club chairman chats with fans online" isn't a particularly tasty morsel but makes for a mildly amusing titbit.

Now well and truly on the hook, our lurking tabloid friends had their snouts in the virtual trough for something a bit more racy, no doubt hoping for some of the sort of stuff their readers had become accustomed to seeing about the club, however inaccurate. Booze-fuelled violence being the main dish on the menu. They didn't get it, but what they did find the next time they logged on was certainly great for a scoop.

A pinned post on Controversial Corner (that's one that remains at the top of the page, being deemed something of importance) revealed that exciting discussions were at an advanced stage for a lucrative sponsorship deal.

Cleverly, rather than make it too obvious, the gist of the post wasn't to simply break a story, but to gauge fan opinion on one of the critical points of it.

It was revealed that Theo was good mates with Easyjet's Stelios and the two entrepreneurs had come up with a typically unique PR exercise that would provide Millwall with its biggest ever commercial sponsorship deal and further push the Easyjet brand. It went on to explain that the one condition of the deal, which was expected to be signed in time for the next season, was that the club wear an orange away kit, as befitting the airline's distinctive branding.

In the current era of luminous pink or marker pen yellow outfits, an orange kit is nothing to raise an eyebrow over, but back in 2000 at Millwall, where fans were still split by Paphitis' change to an all white home kit and its 'Pattycake Lions' badge, for many fans it was the final straw.

There was outrage that Paphitis was going too far, trashing the proud history of the club, turning it into a laughing stock and selling its soul, insisting that Millwall should play in blue at home and red away, or if they had to keep the all white kit, at least keep the original blue for away matches as they had at the time. Fears were raised that this was the thin end of the wedge and their beloved blue would be banished forever, replaced by the latest corporate branding adaptation.

"What's next?" one responder ranted, "Will we have to have a f***ing purple kit cos Theo likes Prince?".

A handful of long-standing HoFers were in on the gag, helping to give it credibility by adding to the debate's outrage and of course, with Paphitis himself having only just recently been on the forum, it had more than the required amount of substance. It's highly likely that Theo was in on the joke himself, but never confirmed.

It worked like a dream. As the desired authenticity was secured with genuine responses to what fans also thought was a real story, the power of PMs (private messages) between Neve and the hardcore HoF membership meant that the true motives behind it were quickly established by the genuine Hof community, who sat back and waited. They weren't disappointed.

The next day, *The Daily Star* ran not just their usual single

Daydreams & Nightmares - Millwall FC in the 2000s - Part 1

par snippet, but a half page lead exclusive - with pictures about how Easjyet's Stelios had persuaded Milllwall to wear an orange kit in return for a sponsorship deal that had both parties fuming. The piece contained some clearly made up responses from Easyjet staff who were less than happy at being associated with a club that was, in their eyes, only known for a riot in the same Luton location that was their HQ. What a horrible own goal by Stelios!

Once out there in print, the HoF piece was swiftly taken down, as if it had never been there - such is the deliciously delete-able nature of the online beast. Whilst the paper piece rapidly became tomorrow's chip paper, the author's embarrassment almost certainly disappearing as quickly as his post-shift pint, Paul and the small legion of Millwall fans that inhabited HoF could definitely afford themselves the quiet satisfaction of having put one over the press for once.

The McGhee debate never reached those levels of publicity, but the overriding opinion was that Millwall had taken a backwards step, Theo had shown a similar naivety that had prompted his appointment of Billy Bonds three years before and the new man was about as loyal as a soap opera lothario who wold jump ship as soon as a better offer came along.

Even Paul Neve couldn't know for sure whether or not Mark McGhee was a HoF lurker. He did know that, during his managerial hiatus, he had started an online venture so was certainly web-savvy.

Earlier in the year McGhee had launched www.thecarbootsale.com and was chairman of the Shrewsbury-based business. Interviewed by *The Birmingham Post and Mail* at the time he said:

"There are millions of people buying and selling second hand goods every weekend across the country - through local papers, in markets and at car boot sales. But there

is no site of this kind on the Internet, a site that anyone can access where they can buy or sell anything they want - thecarbootsale.com will, I believe, fill that gap. Everyone wants to find a bargain and thecarbootsale.com allows you to find that bargain without ever leaving your home."

It's just as well he took the Millwall job. I mean, people buying and selling second hand stuff online?

Ridiculous, it'd never catch on...

If this rather odd story made Millwall fans even more sceptical about McGhee's focus on the job of getting their ninth-placed Lions to the top of the table, they were soon to be reassured.

Daydreams & Nightmares - Millwall FC in the 2000s - Part 1

5. A New Broom

October 2000
1 October - Reggie Kray dies from cancer at a hotel in Norwich aged 66; 4 October - After 41 years, production of the Mini ends at the Longbridge plant owned by MG Rover in Birmingham; 7 October - Wembley Stadium closes after seventy-seven years. It is set to reopen in 2003, following a complete reconstruction that will see its seating capacity raised to 90,000 all-seated. In the final game at the old stadium, the England football team loses 1-0 to Germany in their opening qualifying game for the 2002 World Cup and manager Kevin Keegan resigns after eighteen months in charge. He is succeeded by Swede Sven-Göran Eriksson; The music charts are dominated by All Saints, Steps, The Spice Girls - and U2...

The best way to silence your critics is with actions rather than words and this is never truer than at Millwall. Mark McGhee said all the right things to the press following his appointment but was wisely reticent about making bullish promises. Perhaps conscious that he had queered his pitch at Reading and Leicester and had some image rebuilding to do, it couldn't have began better.

Fickle football fans forgive and forget. Three games into his tenure The Den was awash with amnesia as McGhee's inherited Millwall side chalked up three successive wins with freescoring displays at Posh (4-1) and at home to Bury (4-0) which sandwiched a thoroughly professional 1-0 job at Luton.

Loan star Parkin continued to impress, getting on the scoresheet at Peterborough and giving The Lions a first-minute lead against Bristol City at The Den. Even a late equaliser preventing them from making it five wins from five since the departure of Stevens and McLeary didn't seem to dampen spirits. Fans at The Den for that 1-1 draw were surprised to see chairman Theo Paphitis helping out behind the food and drink kiosk beneath the Cold Blow Lane stands. In what was to prove the start of Paphitis' rise to national recognition and a regular on our television screens, he was filming an episode of a BBC documentary series called *Back to the Floor* where company bosses experience life amongst their workforce and come face to face with the daily trials and tribulations within their business that they may well be blissfully unaware of sat behind their desk or in the boardroom.

Paphitis was typically charismatic, chatting to supporters as if he was just another burger flipper or beer pourer and visibly enjoying the moment the penny dropped: *"Oh, hang on, oh hello, it's you, it's Theo, oi oi!"*

The programme, which aired a few weeks later, also showed Paphitis getting into some trouble by allowing one of his kiosk staff team take home the leftover food that went unsold, only to have his wrists slapped for breaking health and safety regulations.

Another scene - filmed at the previous home match against Bury, would have some implications at the return match later that season and, in what was certainly the most entertaining episode of the entire series, see some bizarre goal celebration scenes at Bournemouth and a tabloid journalist getting the telling off of his life. But more about that later.

Millwall fans were in something of a quandary. Obviously they didn't want McGhee to fail, and their scepticism could be kept alive by the assertion that the scot had simply inherited a fantastic squad - something which, to be fair to McGhee, he freely admitted. However, they had to admit there was a sharpness and new edge to the team now, something that had been lacking under Stevens and McLeary. Whoever was taking the credit, the league table showed it was due with The Lions now sat nicely in third place.

Even the first defeat when it came in the next match at Stoke showed promising signs. At a venue where Millwall rarely fared well, Harris had given them a first minute lead only for The Potters to fight back and lead within thirteen. Harris restored parity right on half time and came agonisingly close to his third hat-trick for the club in the second half fightback only for Chris Iwelumo to deprive them at least a point with a last-kick winner. It was to prove Sam Parkin's last game for the club, returning to parent club Chelsea with no chance of the west London club being prepared to entertain a permanent deal.

Unbowed, they returned to winning ways in the next match when fit again Richard Sadlier stepped into Parkin's boots and scored both in the 2-0 away win over Swindon. This was followed up by another double strike in the 3-1 home win over Cambridge, Harris getting the other goal as Millwall raced to a 3-0 advantage within the half hour with the strike partnership of Harris and Sadlier already looking mouth-wateringly lethal for Lions fans.

November started with a typical Millwall away wobble, another disappointment in the Potteries saw a 1-1 draw with lowly Port Vale and yet another 0-1 reverse against their new nemesis in Wigan, but Paul Moody's return to the side to deputise for the unlucky Sadlier who was struggling with niggling injury once more saw the veteran frontman score the only goal in the 1-0 home win against Wrexham.

Moody also found the net in the routine 3-0 removal of non-league Leigh RMI from the FA Cup first round and the month was rounded off with two gutsy away wins at Bristol Rovers and Oldham. Cahill scored the only goal of the game at a typically bleak Boundary Park. It was a win that underlined the new layer of resilience of this team that had now chalked up eight successes in Mark McGhee's first dozen league matches in charge, making the leap from ninth place when he arrived to the summit ahead of the first match of December at surprise promotion challengers Rotherham.

Ronnie Moore was something of a Rotherham talisman. As a player he joined The Millers in 1980 when they were a mid-table Third Division side who had spent over a dozen seasons in the doldrums. He went on to score 52 goals in 125 appearances as they won the Division Three title in his first season and only missed out on promotion to the top flight by four points in his second. He arrived as manager in 1997 with the club back in the bottom division and guided them to an ultimately unsuccessful play-off place in his first year in charge, going one better by winning promotion as runners up in 99/00. Moore's impressive side defied the pre-season tipsters who felt Division Two would be too tough for them and had mounted a serious campaign for back to back promotions, credentials that would be scrutinised by McGhee's newly table-topping Lions.

A drab opening at a packed Millmoor exploded into life in the second half when Rotherham's David Artell headed his side into the lead within four minutes of the restart. Millwall roared back and a crisp long-range effort from Steven Reid six minutes later made it 1-1. Reid was quickly building a reputation for the power and accuracy of his shooting and both qualities were on show again on 62 minutes when an Ifill cross was only cleared as far as the waiting midfielder on the edge of the area and he showed brilliant composure to tee himself up for another exquisite low shot into the Rotherham net to make it 2-1 and seemingly tighten Millwall's grip on the match - and top spot in the table.

Parity was restored just eight minutes later - but in controversial circumstances. What was clearly a Millwall throw deep in their own half was inexplicably awarded to the home side and Artell sent a howitzer of a long throw into The Lions' penalty area which was only partially cleared. As the ball looped around the despairing Warner in the Millwall goal it broke for Rotherham top scorer Alan Lee on the right had post who steered the ball home to make it 2-2.

With just three minutes remaining Moore's side enjoyed the luck of the devil once again when another throw-in from exactly the same spot was sent in short. The cross was sent over deep to Warner's far post from the edge of the area and Lee's header appeared to hang in the air above Warner for an age, finally landing on top of the bar and then at the feet of a grateful Mark Robins who seemed certain to hook it into the net from point blank range.

A gallant block by young defender Joe Dolan seemed to have let Millwall off the hook but in another twist of fate that confirmed it was to be Rotherham's day, the ball span wildly back across the face of goal, avoiding three covering Lions defenders and straight into the path of Lee who could scarcely believe his luck as he hammered it home for a late winner.

A double distraction in the shape of home cup matches stood between Millwall and the chance to regain top spot from the team that had taken it off them - Walsall - after the midlanders had taken advantage of that surprise Rotherham reverse. Fans were treated to the rare sight of a winger scoring a hat-trick with Christophe Kinet's treble in the 4-1 LDV Trophy tie at a chilly, sparsely populated midweek Den. It wouldn't be the last treble by a Lions wideman that season, and the next was to prove much more spectacular and significant. This was followed by a less inspiring FA Cup second round goalless stalemate with Wycombe.

Goals from Bircham and Reid at the start of each half against Walsall in front of an encouraging pre-Christmas attendance of over 11,000, pushed Millwall back up to second place ahead of the trip to Bournemouth the following week in the last match before Christmas.

In the intervening days, Paphitis' TV debut aired and Millwall exited the FA Cup at the second round stage. With thoughts very much on promotion, the disappointment of once again failing to reach the potentially lucrative third round stage was considerably easier to stomach than in previous seasons. It was the players' stomachs that was one of the many talking points in the aftermath of the first broadcast of *Back to the Floor* however.

In one scene at the club's training ground, Paphitis was dismayed to learn that the players were give free toast as a mid-training snack. Comparing them to cosseted, spoilt kids, the Lions' chairman decided that they would have a subsidised canteen as the employees of his other businesses had - rather than a totally free one.

In a scene that looked ever-so-slightly contrived, star striker Neil Harris was seen to voice his disdain at the decision to make him fork out for his hot buttered sustenance. It was a lighthearted skit that made for more enjoyable viewing than some of the other more mundane episodes and Theo Paphitis came across very well, showing glimpses of the Theo that would become a regular on *Dragons' Den* a few years later, but it earned one unsuspecting journalist an unexpected rollocking.

The Sunday Sport's Martin Fricker had picked up on the scene and ran a lighthearted piece along the lines of: *"Tight- fisted Football Chairman Makes Players Pay For Own Toast"*. Unfortunately for Fricker, Theo didn't see the funny side.

Calling the paper, he furiously demanded to speak to Fricker. Journalists are a tight-knit bunch and look after their own, shielding them from such confrontation, keen to protect the integrity of their fellow hacks. They also like to see their colleagues ripped to shreds and laugh about it in the pub later, so the call was instantly transferred to Martin who was sat at his desk, totally oblivious to the tirade that was about to be unleashed on him.

The young reporter may have already had his fair share of the hairdryer treatment from various chief-editors in his short career, but nothing that would have compared to the tonge-lashing from Theo. As he tried to stutter out some form of apology, his colleagues, scattered around him in the large open plan office, began to get the gist of what it was all about and one by one dissolved into laughter.

Stifling his own amusement, the editor-in-chief summoned Fricker to his desk to ask what it was all about and he sheepishly explained how Paphitis wanted some form of retraction or apology - something no newspaper enjoys.

No doubt at the other end of the line after he had hung up, the mercurial Millwall chairman must have had a mischievous grin on his face too.

The upshot was, by way of a reconciliation, The Sport, in its own inimitable *Carry On* house style that was infinitely more acceptable back in 2000, sent two glamour models to the training ground the next day. The scantily-clad girls were photographed handing out plates of toast to goggle-eyed players who were no doubt praying their wives or girlfriends didn't get to see a copy of the next day's edition.

In a feature unashamedly littered with double entendres such as *'fantastic pair up front'* etc. It is of course, a piece that will not have aged well. Alongside the raucous training ground pictures, face was saved and Paphitis assuaged, with of course, a little bit more publicity for himself and the club. But it wasn't to be the last of Toastgate...

Two days before Christmas, an open terrace on the south coast is not the cosiest of places to spend a Saturday afternoon, but there was plenty to warm the travelling Millwall faithful at Dean Court when Christophe Kinet gave their team the lead with a goal four minutes before half time.

On-loan West Ham youngster Jermaine Defoe had been on an incredible run of scoring in successive matches for The Cherries and he continued with the equaliser ten minutes into the second half.

But with twenty minutes remaining, the scene was set for the perfect end to what had been one of the more bizarre weeks in Millwall's recent history.

A long Tony Warner clearance was won in the air on the edge of the box by Paul Moody and it fell perfectly for the onrushing Neil Harris to deftly slide the ball past the advancing 'keeper in front of the celebrating Lions fans, As Harris ran to the perimeter fence to celebrate with them, slices of toast looped through the air in his direction.

Fortunately, the press didn't take the predictable angle of accusing *"Millwall's notorious hooligan element of showering the pitch with missiles"* no matter how hard that cold toast must have been. But then with Theo Paphitis fighting the club's corner now, it's not surprising.

Millwall fans could enjoy their Christmas knowing their team were top of the table once more, and looking good to add the Division Two title to their trophy cabinet in the new year:

Nationwide League Division 2 - Dec 23rd 2000						
	P	W	D	L	F	A	PTS
1. MILLWALL	**21**	**13**	**3**	**5**	**40**	**19**	**42**
2. Wigan	21	11	9	1	29	17	42
3. Walsall	21	12	5	4	37	21	41
4. Rotherham	20	12	4	5	37	26	40

So far Millwall had stuck to the formula that usually guarantees success - two points per game. But with just two points separating the top four, the promotion race was anything but run and promised to be even tighter than the previous campaign. Millwall knew from that bitter experience that the teams topping the table the previous Christmas weren't able to stay there so they would need to increase the pressure on the chasing pack - especially with Wigan due to visit The Den for the first home match of the New Year.

But with two Den clashes against mid-table opposition still to play in the current year, focus was on ending it with maximum points.

The first was straightforward enough as The Lions' already impressive goal difference was given a huge boost in the 6-0 Boxing Day drubbing of Colchester with a Neil Harris hat-trick, Paul Moody brace and Ifill strike past the hapless Andy Woodman in the Essex side's goal.

Four days later Notts County arrived as Millwall aimed to end the year on a high note with a third successive league win since that Rotherham defeat. Other festive results had gone The Lions' way and they started the match with a four point lead over second-placed Walsall. The Magpies didn't read the memo however and took a sixth-minute lead through Hughes, Ifill grabbed an equaliser ten minutes later but it was Hughes again in the 36th minute to restore the visitors' shock lead.

A breathless first half continued with Moody making it

2-2 just two minutes later, and the two teams went into the break all square.

A less eventful second half appeared to be petering out to a frustrating draw, The Lions' attack blunted by the sending off of Christophe Kinet. But just as Millwall fans were counting the cost of only collecting a point, Gary Owers struck a last-minute winner for County to end Millwall's year on a whimper rather than a bang and McGhee's first home defeat. Such is the nature of English football at the turn of any year, after playing three matches in a week, Millwall would now have seven days to wait for the next match, and then face three matches in a seven day spell again.

A trip to face promotion rivals Reading was next, followed by home matches against Swindon in the LDV Trophy and what would undoubtedly be the biggest game of the season so far: second-placed Wigan.

Reading, like Rotherham, were one of the surprise challengers for the top spots and their charge into the top six had been fuelled on an excellent home record at The Madejski Stadium. Their record of nine wins and just one draw and defeat from eleven home games was the best in the division and they were the biggest goalscorers too. McGhee returned to the club where he carved his managerial reputation knowing that this could possibly be as stiff a test as the visit of Wigan a week later.

Millwall couldn't afford to lose focus now.

When Neil Harris tapped home Millwall's second goal in just the 22nd minute at Reading, the travelling Lions fans were wondering what all the fuss was about. It had followed another typical Harris strike five minutes earlier when he hooked home the first from inside the six yard box.

Harris' stock as an lethal striker was gaining with every

match. He clearly possessed that instinct that all good goalscorers need which is to fashion a scoring opportunity out of seemingly nothing before the defenders realise the threat.

By the half hour mark it was three as former Lion Ricky Newman turned the ball into his own net and thoughts were now turning to another rout like the Boxing Day drubbing of Colchester.

It was certainly on the cards when, five minutes into the second half, Harris was impeded in the Reading box and he dusted himself off to despatch the spot kick and grab his second hat-trick in three matches and third of the season to start the comparisons with Lions goalscoring legend Teddy Sheringham who managed four trebles during his record-breaking final season two decades before.

By the time Reading were awarded a penalty of their own with fifteen minutes left, Sammy Igoe had headed a 65th minute consolation and Jamie Cureton's third for Reading with literally the last kick of the match made the scoreline look far closer than the 90 minutes had been. Not only did Reading lose the match, they lost their stadium announcer too. In an attempt to fire up the fans prematch, the overzealous PA man made comments about Mark McGhee, forcing Reading to issue an official apology, and the announcer to resign leaving red faces all round for The Royals.

There were certainly no complaints about Millwall's next defeat, an exit on penalties in the LDV Trophy at home to Swindon after a goalless 120 minutes in front of just over 2,000 fans at a cold, echoey Den. McGhee's men now had a clear sight of the finish line with no distractions.

The atmosphere was more raucous for the visit of Wigan four days later where over 15,000 fans were doused in winter sunshine, with the vast majority hoping to see

Millwall end a mini hoodoo over a Wigan side that they hadn't managed to beat in their previous six meetings.

Just as at Reading, Millwall made the perfect start, with two Paul Moody goals in the first 26 minutes. The first was a typically dominant towering header, the second getting on the end of a perfect Neil Harris cross.

The second half saw Moody complete his hat-trick in what was becoming a history-making season - and an expensive one for Millwall who must have been running out of match balls by now - with this the third in four league matches for The Lions' rampant frontmen. A late consolation for Wigan who had been reduced to ten men with the sending off of striker Haworth didn't dampen the euphoria of finally beating their Lancastrian rivals. Sad news filtered from The Den during the following week however with news that former Lion Johnny Hartburn had died. He scored 30 goals in 112 appearances for the club during the early part of the fifties.

Mid-table Bournemouth arrived at The Den having been part of a little bit of history. Their on-loan striker Jermaine Defoe - who had continued his goalscoring streak against The Lions in their 2-1 win at Dean Court just before Christmas - had kept on scoring and, during the week at Cambridge, netted in his tenth consecutive league match to equal a post-war record.

That record was to end at The Den, but not in the way Millwall fas would have wanted. The Jekyll and Hyde side of McGhee's team was once again in evidence when they went from notching up fifteen goals and three hat-tricks in four matches to not being able to find a way past a Bournemouth defence that managed to protect Claus Jorgensen's sixth-minute opener and send The Lions spinning to a fourth home defeat of the season with a little over half of it played.

For once, it was Millwall's away form that impressed, having recorded eight wins and only three losses on the road. The frustration for fans - and I'm sure McGhee - was that had their team been able to show the sort of invincibility at home that the club had made their hallmark over the years, they'd have been out of sight at the top of the table by now, instead they had now been dislodged at the summit for the first time in six weeks by Walsall.

But since when did Millwall ever do anything the easy way?

Thankfully the goals began to flow again in February as a routine 3-0 defeat of Bristol Rovers at The Den with goals from Cahill, Moody and Harris, but there was still bad news as young defender Joe Dolan suffered a broken leg following a clash with fellow defender Robbie Ryan, ending the centre back's season after he had made the place his own since November.

Fortunately McGhee had the experience of Stuart Nethercott to call on. The former Spurs man was a solid replacement and slotted in perfectly next to Sean Dyche at the heart of The Lions' defence. The match had also seen a change in goal for Millwall with Willy Gueret a surprise replacement for Tony Warner.

It wasn't without controversy either. Two minutes after giving his side the lead, Cahill, who had just returned to the starting lineup after a one-match suspension for accruing five yellow cards, was given a straight red for an off the ball incident with Rovers' Dwayne Plummer. With play halted after Rovers were awarded a free kick, Cahill threw the ball at Plummer who retaliated by slapping him in the face. Both players were sent off and Millwall would be without their influential midfielder for four matches in the middle of the crucial run-in.

Three days later Millwall travelled to Colchester with

the match only confirmed during the afternoon. The Layer Road surface had been unplayable for 45 days following rain which had led to the original match between the sides being called off.

The Lions were in desperate need for the game to go ahead so as to take full advantage of at least one of their two games in hand.

Thankfully it did and on a surface that reduced the football that both sides attempted to play on it to nothing more than a medieval-type display of hoofing chunks of mud around, Millwall were able to grind out a priceless 1-0 victory thanks to a Paul Ifill goal midway through the first half. It was every but as valuable as the 6-0 win over the Essex side six weeks earlier at The Den - and those wins against promotion rivals Reading and Wigan.

It wasn't just the Colchester playing surface that was giving cause for concern though. The Den pitch had come in for criticism from both manager and fans and was so bad that McGhee admitted he had to change his tactics for the match with Wigan because of it.

The proactive Paphitis cancelled the contract of the club's current company and brought in former Manchester City groundsman David Shaw. But pitches can't be put right overnight and it was made clear that whilst nothing could be done in the middle of a busy season, by the time the next campaign arrived the Den surface would see a marked improvement. Now it was up to Mark McGhee and his team to make sure they were playing Division One football on it.

A goalless draw away to relegation-haunted Swansea wasn't the end of the world (in fact it was the end of a remarkable run that hadn't seen Millwall involved in a goalless league draw for 60 matches). Neither was it enough to knock Millwall off top spot, but it was frustrating nevertheless that The Lions had once again failed to beat a struggling side. They came close, but Harris' goal was ruled out for a foul on the Swans' 'keeper.

It did provide new Lions stopper Willy Gueret with his third clean sheet in three matches with Mark McGhee admitting that the decision to drop the popular Scouse stopper Warner had been a hard one, but that he was keen to see if the Frenchman from Guadeloupe was a credible deputy - which so far he had proved beyond doubt.

It was another example of the strength in depth of this Millwall side who still had firepower back up to call upon, with unlucky striker Richard Sadlier making his way back into contention as a regular goalscorer for the reserves and getting an invaluable 90 first team minutes in south Wales. His return to first team action would soon prove to be pivotal in Millwall's promotion hopes.

The Sky Sports cameras were at The Den to provide live coverage of the Friday night 1-0 victory over Brentford thanks to a typical Tim Cahill goal, underlining just how much Millwall would miss him during his enforced four match absence after that match. Brentford had done a good job of keeping The Lions' lethal strikeforce quiet, but were unable to extend that vigilance to the ever-dangerous Cahill. Meanwhile, Tony Warner must have been growing increasingly concerned about when he might be able to claim his first team place back as Gueret was yet to concede a goal in his four league appearances.

All that was to change though...

With Moody and Harris goals in the opening quarter of each half putting Millwall seemingly in complete control at Northampton, Willy Gueret's dream start to life with The Lions was about to turn into a bit of a nightmare, but through no fault of his own.

First the evergreen Marco Gabbiadini was able to squeeze

the ball through a forest of Lions legs on the hour mark to make it 2-1, then seven minutes later defender Matt Lawrence conceded the first of two penalties as the match turned completely on its head. The first appeared harsh, Lawrence seeming to merely tangle legs with the Cobblers' attacker as both made legitimate attempts to win the ball. But he could have few complaints with the second when he felled Forrester after the striker had jinked his way around the Millwall right-back.

Both penalties were despatched by ex Lion Dave Savage and, with just three minutes remaining, Millwall were looking at a potentially costly 2-3 defeat. Fortunately they were able to make it six goals at Sixfields - from the most unlikeliest of headed sources.

A long throw was headed on for the diminutive Christophe Kinet to arrive and power a header into the net from close range to send the travelling Lions fans behind the goal mad.

Four days later Millwall made another short trip outside the capital to Oxford where a goal from Us' old boy Moody and Dave Livermore saw Millwall return to winning ways again with a 2-0 victory. The Lions went into a very busy March with almost half of their remaining matches crammed into the month where the transfer window would slam shut.

Little did Mark McGhee know just how valuable the work he did in that window would be to Millwall's promotion dream...

6. Beware the sides of March

March 2001...
8 March – The wreckage of Donald Campbell's speedboat Bluebird K7 is raised from the bottom of Coniston Water in Cumbria, 34 years after Campbell was killed in an attempt to break the world water speed record. His body is recovered one week later; New TV reality show 'Popstars' creates a new group Hear'Say, who reach number one with their debut single. It begins two decades of similar shows culminating in The X Factor which would run for 15 series from 2004...

The old gag about London buses was in evidence at The Den for Millwall's first match of March, but there were few smiles as Lions fans left the stadium. After 60 matches without a league 0-0, Millwall had now managed two in five, the latest being a frustrating stalemate with Peterborough. It meant McGhee's team had managed just two wins from their last five matches and yet in complete contrast to the period of the season when, despite a string of victories were unable to shake off the attentions of Wigan and Walsall breathing down their necks, this relatively bleak spell had seen them open up a six point lead at the top of the table.

With Walsall and Wigan also losing form, it was Rotherham

who had emerged as The Lions' main challengers for the top spot and The Millers must have been encouraged by the alarming wobble that Millwall seemed to be experiencing, which continued with the midweek trip to Bury.

Neil Harris gave his side a fourth minute lead at Gigg Lane, but a Cramb equaliser on the half hour and a Newby winner with the last kick of the match sent Millwall spinning to their first defeat in nine. The match was also to see yet more fallout from the *Back to the Floor* programme. When it was aired, chairman Theo Paphitis was seen to be surveying the carnage of the visitors' toilets following the 4-0 home win over Bury. The travelling fans had clearly decided to take out their frustrations on The Den facilities with smashed porcelain and pipework lying in pools of water. With this broadcast to the viewing public, it must have come as no surprise to the Bury ground staff when they entered the toilets at their own visitors' enclosure after their late victory against The Lions to see a similar scene of destruction.

The absence of Cahill had proved costly. His four match ban had seen Millwall win one, draw two and lose one. Without him, teams seemed to be able to snuff out The Lions' multiple goal threats, whereas with Cahill, their best form of defence was attack, without him they were often on the back foot.

Cahill's return did indeed herald a return to winning ways with a rare Nethercott goal earning a hard-fought 1-0 victory over relegation-bound Luton at The Den but the next match - a Friday night trip to Bristol City's Ashton Gate - was to prove more damage to Millwall's promotion push and see them knocked off the top of the table.

When Harris converted a penalty on the hour mark to cancel out Carey's first half opener for The Robins, the travelling Lions fans felt the game was there for the taking.

Instead it exploded into life in the final minutes, seemingly depriving Millwall of their two main strikers for the most critical stage of the season.

First City's Thorpe was shown a straight red for a kick out on Dyche in retaliation as Bristol won a free kick on the right hand side. While the home side prepared to take the set piece, Moody and Beadle tangled in the area and, after a lengthy deliberation, fans on both sides were incredulous as referee Jones showed both players a red card.

Finally the farce was complete when a 90th-minute attack by Bristol City saw the ball hammered at Dyche who could nothing to prevent the ball striking his arm. In what was a clear example of accidental handball with his arms by his side, the linesman instantly drew his flag across his chest and ref Jones pointed to the spot. Matthews duly obliged and Millwall had been beaten again. There was still time for a furious Neil Harris to receive a straight red card in the final chaotic seconds meaning The Lions would be deprived of their two top scorers for four of the final nine matches.

Millwall needed firepower, and they needed it now. Not only were Rotherham continuing their upward momentum, taking over from The Lions at the top of the table, but now Reading were hitting form too. Fans were starting to have a recurring nightmare of the previous season when their promotion hopes fell apart in a few expensive weeks.

McGhee had almost three weeks to prepare for the next match - a midweek trip to Wycombe - by which time he had attempted to cushion the blow of losing Moody and Harris by recruiting veteran striker Tony Cottee. It was a less than inspiring addition for Millwall fans, who mistrusted the acquisition of ex West Ham players at the best of times and his appearance as sub in the third goalless draw in nine matches did little to inspire.

Twenty four hours later the transfer window closed - as was its traditional date of the last Thursday in March back then. McGhee was able to make one more addition to his frontline and this time the reaction from fans was far more favourable.

Steve Claridge had, to use the age-old cliché - had more clubs than Jack Niklaus, but more significantly had scored prolifically at almost every one. He was, in theory, the perfect Millwall footballer. A grafter who not only rolled his sleeves up, but his socks down..

It brought to an end a thoroughly miserable month that could have seen Millwall all but rubber stamp promotion. Six matches had yielded just six points, The Lions worst return of the season at its most crucial juncture. Had they lost their bottle at the worst possible time once more?

With Rotherham appearing to be on course to take the title, holding a three point lead over The Lions, and Reading just a point behind with a game in hand, it felt like promotion was, once again, slipping through Millwall's fingers with the prospect of another play-off campaign looming and the spectre of Wigan hovering ominously in the top six:

Nationwide League Division 2 - March 31st 2001

	P	W	D	L	F	A	PTS
1. Rotherham	39	23	8	8	72	49	77
2. MILLWALL	**39**	**22**	**8**	**9**	**70**	**36**	**74**
3. Reading	38	22	7	9	70	41	73
4. Walsall	39	19	10	10	67	43	67
5. Wigan	40	16	17	7	46	34	65
6. Stoke	39	17	13	9	63	42	64

7. Daydream Believers

April 2001...15 April - Manchester United win the FA Premier League title for the third season in succession, and the seventh time in nine seasons, then pay a British record fee of £19million for Ruud van Nistelrooy;
May 2001... 12 May - Liverpool win the FA Cup Final when two Michael Owen goals in the final minutes of the game give them a 2-1 win over Arsenal in the final at the Millennium Stadium; 16 May - Deputy Prime Minister John Prescott punches a protester who threw an egg at him in Rhyl; Liverpool win the UEFA Cup - their first European trophy for 17 years - with a 5-4 win over Spanish side Deportivo Alavés...

The last thing Millwall really needed at this stage of the season was to face a side who were turning a late run of form into scrapping for a play-off place. Stoke were, as they had been the previous season, that team. With Warner restored to the first team for the 0-0 draw at Walsall, the midweek Den clash also saw Claridge make his first Millwall bow.

Fortunately for McGhee, not only did the experience of Claridge in his 88-minute debut provide some much-needed stability and composure that had gone missing in recent weeks, the fit-again Sadlier was able to thrive next to his new strike partner. Nerves were eased early on when Sadlier gave Millwall a sixth-minute lead and The Potters rarely troubled the home side as Cahill sealed the points with a goal ten minutes from time. It wasn't pretty, but the main thing was to get back to winning football matches to try and salvage a top two place. It was ideal preparation for the next match at The Den four days later: leaders Rotherham.

A packed Den provided a deafening backdrop for the meeting of second versus first. Rotherham had come from nowhere to the verge of adding the Division Two title to their Third Division runners-up spot the previous season.

The Millers had gained a reputation for steamrollering opponents with their direct style of play - something that was in evidence in the late 2-3 capitulation when the teams met earlier in the season so a quick start was vital for McGhee's men.

That was exactly what they got when, after a bit of pinball in the Rotherham six yard box in the 13th minute, Cahill was able to hammer home to make it 1-0 and send The Den into raptures.

The lead was doubled on the half hour mark when Steven Reid produced a similar strike to the two he had scored in the first match. Picking his spot and guiding the ball home at pace with a pinpoint shot from just outside the area.

The game was virtually over as a contest moments later when shellshocked Rotherham tried to regain a foothold in the match and key striker Alan Lee let frustration get the better of him. His foul on Reid as the Millwall midfielder tormented the lumbering striker earned him a straight red and ended the visitors' hopes of getting back into the game.

With the shackles off, it was time for a new hero to be inducted into the Millwall Hall of Fame. Livermore's cross five minutes before half time was headed onto the top of the bar and the ever-alert Claridge was on hand to poach his first goal for the club in what would go on to be a three year love affair between player and club.

Less than two matches into his Lions career, Claridge cemented his place into its folklore nine minutes into the second half when he collected a Matt Lawrence pass with his back to the Rotherham goal 25 yards out. He jinked and turned his marker brilliantly sending a glorious effort into the top corner of the net to send the crowd wild once more and seal one of the most impressive victories in Millwall's recent history.

It was enough to take Millwall back to the top of the league and, with two more home matches to come in the next seven days, a second chance to seal promotion that they thought may have been passing them by.

With Moody and Harris now available, McGhee had an embarrassment of riches up front once more. It was Sadlier, who had emerged from a season punctuated by injury, who was to show his worth as another visit from The Potteries saw him net a first half winner against Port Vale. It was a million miles from the sparkling display against Rotherham however as Vale spurned numerous chances to cancel out The Lions' opener.

Harris made a return to the side from the bench after an hour of a nervy encounter at home to Swindon next and within 60 seconds he was back in business curling home a beautiful shot from the edge of the area as Millwall ground out their second 1-0 win in a row and made it four wins on the bounce.

The value of those four wins - no doubt boosted by them all being at home - was borne out by the table which showed Millwall still had some work to do to get themselves over the line. Rotherham were just three points behind and Reading five - both with a game in hand. Fortunately goal difference was in Millwall's favour - thanks in no small part to that blitzing of The Millers - so if it did come down to the wire, that was worth an extra point. Although whether Millwall fans' hearts were up to that as they went into the final three matches of the season was up for debate.

Three days later that goal difference was all that was keeping Millwall on top after Rotherham had won 1-0 at home to Northampton 24 hours earlier. With Reading playing at Oxford while Millwall travelled to Cambridge, it promised to be a real education into who would finally win promotion.

More early nerves were calmed at The Abbey Stadium when Stuart Nethercott rose majestically to head home a 37th minute cross against a Cambridge side battling relegation - the sort of opposition usually so dangerous to Millwall sides in recent seasons.

Then, seven minutes into the second half, brilliant work by Reid on the left hand side saw his cross only partially cleared and so began the Paul Ifill show.

His sweet volley from the edge of the box sealed the points - despite Youngs giving Cambridge an unlikely lifeline that they never looked like capitalising on, and another from Claridge on 74 made it three.

Sadly that would be Claridge's last contribution of the season after he was injured later in the match.

More Reid trickery on the left led to Ifill blasting home his second with a sweet left foot half-volley.

Two minutes later the same two players - who had come through the Millwall academy together - combined once more to put the seal on the match and one of the best hat-tricks ever scored by a Lions player.

Reid marauded through the centre circle into the home side's half and found Ifill out on the left. He cut inside before unleashing an unstoppable shot from 25 yards to complete his first treble for the club and the sixth from four different players that season.

The goal that Millwall had conceded had been the first in 607 minutes and they had now racked up 13 goals in five matches. After all the uncertainty of March that had seen a worrying combination of a leaky defence and shot-shy attack, everything it seemed had clicked into place at just the right time. With Reading winning 2-0 at Oxford, the pressure was still on. But with a three point lead and just two games to go, one win from either the trip to Wrexham or the final match of the season at home to Oldham would be enough when Millwall's goal difference advantage of more than ten goals was factored in.

Both Rotherham and Reading would play their games in hand over The Lions before the trip to north Wales. Optimists on The House of Fun were planning a promotion party outside the closed Den should slip-ups from either hand them promotion without Millwall having to kick a ball. Unfortunately, they were going to have to earn it.

Reading did indeed slip up, drawing 2-2 with Walsall, but Rotherham ensured they would take the title race to the final day with a win over Luton. Mark McGhee's side - and a legion of noisy Millwall fans arrived in Wrexham knowing that a point would be enough to see them back to English football's second tier.

With Wrexham woefully unprepared for the siege from south London, cash was being exchanged at the turnstiles for the all ticket away enclosure and it came as no surprise that, as the game started, the visitors' end was a little overcrowded. It was silenced temporarily when Falcon-bridge stabbed a ninth minute cross beyond Warner and nails were starting to be bitten when news filtered through from Layer Road and Millmoor that Reading were ahead at Colchester and Rotherham were beating Brentford.

By the time referee Cowburn blew for half time however, Reading's nerves had got the better of them and they trailed 1-2. It wasn't an ideal scenario but as it stood, even defeat would see Millwall fans celebrate promotion at the end of the match.

Other scores at half time revealed Crystal Palace trailed against Wolves and, as it stood, were about to swap places with Millwall, prompting chants of: *"Millwall up and Palace down, doo dah, doo dah..."*. In the background, the stadium Tannoy belted out the *Feeder* hit *Buck Rogers* - the chorus of *"I think we're gonna make it..."* seemingly prophetic.

Within eight minutes of the restart Tim Cahill ensured the carnival atmosphere was in full swing when he headed home a corner to make it 1-1 and prompt delirious scenes. It took several minutes to clear the pitch of jubilant travelling fans and whilst Millwall weren't able to virtually assure the title with a second, confirmation of Reading's demise saw the promotion party begin well before the final whistle.

Millwall *had* finally made it. Through those dark days when fans walked away from Bury on the final match of the 96/97 season wondering if they would have a team to support when the new season started, to the painful rebuilding of the club almost from scratch. Finally Millwall could enjoy a final day party like the one they'd walked away from at Gigg Lane four years before. All that was left to do now was claim only their second league title in almost forty years.

As perfect football days go, Saturday May 5th, 2001 was about as good as it gets. A sold out Den where demand was such that home fans were accommodated in the away stand, was bathed in Spring sunshine and awash with flags as The Lions' long-suffering fans soaked up a day they had waited thirteen years for.

The title celebrations were started in fitting style with a Paul Moody goal after 21 minutes and nine minutes later Neil Harris once again showed that he was so much more than just a six yard box poacher with an exquisite chip from the right hand edge of the box to make it two.

The pick of the goals - and possibly one of the best seen at Millwall in many years - came early in the second half when Harris laid the ball back to Reid on the left hand corner of the Oldham box and the impressive young midfielder who had visibly grown as a player in a few short months of that season unleashed an unstoppable shot that almost broke the visitors' net.

The Harris-Moody partnership was back in business again just after the hour mark when the former crossed for the 33-year-old to head home for 4-0.

The only dilemma left was, when Marc Bircham was upended in the penalty area in injury time to leave referee Bates with the easy decision of pointing to the spot:

Who would take the kick?

Moody was on his second hat-trick of the season - and what would have been an incredible seventh in total for Millwall for the season. But Harris, who was in all fairness, The Lions' regular spot-kick taker, was also just one goal away from the Golden Boot.

Harris duly despatched the penalty to give Millwall a 5-0 victory and secure the title in style - along with his 27th league goal of the season, making him the first Lions player to score over 20 goals in a season since Teddy Sheringham's 38-goal haul twenty years before.

The sound of *The Monkees* belted out around the stadium as Millwall's victorious champions took their well-deserved lap of honour. The group's hit *Daydream Believer* had, some years earlier, been sung by Sunderland fans with the lyrics changed to *Cheer Up Peter Reid* in tribute to Reid's success with The Black Cats. It wasn't usually Millwall fans' style to crib other supporters' chants but this was far too tempting as it scanned so well when tweaked to include the name of Mark McGhee.

The manager who had left Millwall fans seriously underwhelmed when he was appointed earlier that season had won them over, even if he had done it with Stevens' and McLeary's side. His managerial nous had clearly taken the team to the next level which had been needed in another close-run league campaign.

As it turned out, both Rotherham and Reading failed to win their final matches, with both draws leaving the final table looking a lot more comfortable than it had felt in those final few matches when all three teams seemed to be matching each other point for point.

The promotion party went on long into the south London night where the presentation podium used for skipper Stuart Nethercott to raise the championship trophy aloft mysteriously disappeared from the centre circle and reappeared later that evening outside a pub on the Old Kent Road.

It was a perfect end to a perfect day - and season.

Sadly, as is often the case in Millwall's history, the unbridalled joy and relief of promotion and success on the pitch was soon to give way to shock and sadness off it with the announcement just days after those celebrations that striker Neil Harris had been diagnosed with cancer.

Daydreams & Nightmares - Millwall FC in the 2000s - Part 1

NATIONWIDE LEAGUE DIVISION TWO
FINAL TABLE 2000/2001

1	**MILLWALL**	**46**	**28**	**9**	**9**	**89**	**38**	**+51**	**93**
2	**Rotherham United**	**46**	**27**	**10**	**9**	**79**	**55**	**+24**	**91**
3	Reading	46	25	11	10	86	52	+34	86
4	**Walsall**	**46**	**23**	**12**	**11**	**79**	**50**	**+29**	**81**
5	Stoke City	46	21	14	11	74	49	+25	77
6	Wigan Athletic	46	19	18	9	53	42	+11	75
7	Bournemouth	46	20	13	13	79	55	+24	73
8	Notts County	46	19	12	15	62	66	−4	69
9	Bristol City	46	18	14	14	70	56	+14	68
10	Wrexham	46	17	12	17	65	71	−6	63
11	Port Vale	46	16	14	16	55	49	+6	62
12	Peterborough United	46	15	14	17	61	66	−5	59
13	Wycombe Wanderers	46	15	14	17	46	53	−7	59
14	Brentford	46	14	17	15	56	70	−14	59
15	Oldham Athletic	46	15	13	18	53	65	−12	58
16	Bury	46	16	10	20	45	59	−14	58
17	Colchester United	46	15	12	19	55	59	−4	57
18	Northampton Town	46	15	12	19	46	59	−13	57
19	Cambridge United	46	14	11	21	61	77	−16	53
20	Swindon Town	46	13	13	20	47	65	−18	52
21	**Bristol Rovers**	**46**	**12**	**15**	**19**	**53**	**57**	**−4**	**51**
22	**Luton Town**	**46**	**9**	**13**	**24**	**52**	**80**	**−28**	**40**
23	**Swansea City**	**46**	**8**	**13**	**25**	**47**	**73**	**−26**	**37**
24	**Oxford United**	**46**	**7**	**6**	**33**	**53**	**100**	**−47**	**27**

Daydreams & Nightmares - Millwall FC in the 2000s - Part 1

we can be heroes...
01/02

Daydreams & Nightmares - Millwall FC in the 2000s - Part 1

Daydreams & Nightmares - Millwall FC in the 2000s - Part 1

8. Perspective...

July & August 2001...
2 July - Barry George is sentenced to life imprisonment for the murder of the television presenter Jill Dando, who was killed in Fulham, London, on 26 April 1999. - George would later be acquitted at a retrial in 2008; 12 July - The British transfer record is broken for the third time in eight months when Manchester United pay Italian club Lazio £28.1million for Argentine midfielder Juan Sebastián Verón;
11 August - Southampton F.C. move into their new 32,000-seat St Mary's Stadium...

Neil Harris was sitting by the pool on the club's summer break, no doubt reflecting on an unforgettable season that had ended with him as not only the top scorer at Millwall - but in the entire country. His hands, as most men's often are - to the regular disgruntlement to their partners no doubt - were rummaging around in his shorts.

Nobody can explain this bizarre habit. I myself have been pulled up on it by my own wife - more often than not I was blissfully unaware that I was even doing it.

"Why *do* men do *that?*" is her regular retort.

Until Harris' diagnosis none of our species could offer an explanation to that question apart from some pithy response. Since then, thanks to the Millwall striker, I at least have a sensible reply. *"I'm just checking everything's OK"*

Soon after that blissful day by the pool, Harris suddenly realised everything was not OK, as he explained in a 2018 interview with *The Sun*'s Paul Jiggins:

"We'd had our end-of-season trip and I was sitting by the pool with my hands down my shorts and felt the lump and just thought nothing of it really.

"I was then back home a few days later laying on the bed watching Only Fools and Horses and checked it again and just thought, 'That doesn't feel right'.

"The difference between the two testicles was quite clear for me. One felt dense and heavy and sort of solid and one felt normal, what I'd always known.

"I immediately phoned the club doctor and booked an appointment."

A scan confirmed Neil had testicular cancer and he said: *"I'll never forget watching the ultrasound.*

"It was the same as when you go for a pregnancy scan with the girlfriend, wife, whatever, the ultrasound was going over the area and I remember seeing one testicle and what it looked like.

"I then remember seeing the other one and, it sounds a bit crazy, but one looked a bit like the Earth from up in the sky when you're looking down and the other one was just like a solid, solid mass.

"I was looking, again naively, and thinking, 'Oh, that's not right'.

"As I left I was taken by the club doctor into a different chamber and told it was testicular cancer.

"The moment you're told your whole word sinks.

"I had three questions to ask the doctor. The first one at the forefront of my mind was, 'Am I going to die?'.

"The doctor had enough knowledge of testicular cancer to say the survival rate was extremely high. I think straight away, from the top of his knowledge, it was like 98 per cent, so it was reassuring to a certain level.

"My next question was, 'Will I be able to play football again?'.

"That was a big question for me. The answer was they didn't know, which stung a bit.

"The third one was, 'Can I have children?' and that was also a 'didn't know'."

Harris added: "I'd just had the most successful year of my life playing football, you feel you're invincible.

"I was 23, scoring goals, happy life, just been promoted to the Championship with Millwall."

Until then, for many people, cancer was still a disease for the old, frail and sickly. Of course you heard of younger, fitter people being struck down by the disease from time to time, but for millions of people - especially male football fans - this was a huge shock. An athlete in the prime of his life, young, fit, being looked after conditionally and nutritionally by his football club, diagnosed with cancer?

Fortunately that initial prognosis was accurate and, after surgery and radiotherapy, Harris was able to concentrate on making a full recovery and go on to have three children. Obviously Millwall fans at the time couldn't help but hang on that second question, but it felt totally inappropriate to speculate when or if they would see Harris scoring goals for The Lions again.

Once more, real life had put mere football into perspective and yet again rubbished those oft-misquoted words of Bill Shankly. It's so easy to get caught up in your team's quest for glory. To live and breathe it every day, to awake thinking about the next match, agonise over the latest defeat or draw and lose yourself in permutations of the games and possible results to come. Then life grabs you by the shoulders and shakes you out of it. Of course football isn't more important than life and death and Shankly himself, were he here today, would indefatigably agree.

Harris' cancer diagnosis would, in the years to come, totally change attitudes towards the disease. The candour with which he spoke about his experience and the fact that so many thousands of men who would not normally have entertained such discussions, along with his Everyman Appeal, undoubtedly changed - and saved - lives.

It was the main topic for discussion as Millwall hosted Spurs at The Den for their final pre-season match before starting life back in English Football's second tier.

The game was arranged as a benefit match for Keith Stevens who had, of course, just 12 months earlier, been preparing the team for the new season as part of his managerial duo with McLeary.

The 16,000 crowd was a testimony to the high esteem that fans still held Rhino in, and was a fitting way to put a collective Millwall arm around him and say: *"No hard feelings mate"*.

On reflection, the club may have admitted that the choice of opposition - who won an entertaining match 2-1 - might have been a little naive with the rivalry between the two teams not being tested since the old First Division days over a decade earlier. Events outside the stadium before and after the match were, not to put to fine a point on it, a little testy!

Mark McGhee's summer transfer activity had been quiet. This was one area where the jury was still out. His acquisition of Steve Claridge - who had thankfully recovered from the injury sustained in that 5-1 win at Cambridge and signed a season-long extension deal - had been a masterstroke. In fact it wouldn't be an exaggeration to say his signing may well have proved the difference between winning the title and possibly missing out altogether. Claridge brought so much more than goals. His experience, composure and mere presence in the dressing room elevated the team (that had lost its two top scorers through suspension at a vital time in the season) from self pity to a rampaging confidence that shot them to the top and kept them there.

Then there was Tony Cottee.

His Wycombe cameo did little to inspire and his presence almost instantly forgotten.

The only new face at The Den was Giovanni Savarese. A 30-year-old, six foot Venezuelan striker who came with an impressive strike rate of more than a goal every other game.

That those goals were scored in his native Venezuela and the lower reaches of the US Soccer leagues - which was really nothing more than UK non-league standard back in the 90s - did little to inspire Lions fans' excitement.

There was always that little hope in the back of your mind that said: *"Hang on, maybe we've unearthed a little diamond here. Someone off the radar, this could be good..."* and you drift off to scenes at the end of the season where Savarese is being chaired off by his teammates having scored his 30th goal of the campaign to clinch promotion to the Premier League in the play off final.

Giovanni Savarese would in fact go on to make one Millwall appearance as a 68th-minute sub, and never been seen at The Den again.

The long-awaited season-opener was at home to Norwich. The Canaries were not the top flight and Championship yo-yo side that they are today and had finished mid-table in each of the five seasons since relegation from the Premier League, so it seemed a perfect way for Millwall to ease their way in. Manager Nigel Worthington had built a side that was considered one to watch this season however so Millwall would surely be tested. As it turned out, The Lions would actually be starting their season against two of the leading protagonists in the end-of-season promotion saga. And they would be closer to that than any Lions fan could have dreamed of.

Any first day nerves were soon dismissed as Millwall simply appeared to be picking up from where they left off. A 12th-minute Claridge strike sent the 14,000 crowd wild as Millwall swarmed all over the Norfolk side from the first whistle.

Claridge was wearing the number 35 - which coincided with his age - but was playing more like a 25-year-old.

More significantly, that number was in white, because it was on a royal blue home shirt. The Lions had returned to their more familiar home kit, much to the majority of fans' delight.

Millwall were back in business, in every way.

Another Reid screamer right on half time had The Den rocking almost as much as it had been for the final home league game against Oldham and the gloss was added to a 4-0 victory courtesy of Tim Cahill and Lucas Neill in the second half.

It was of course far too early to talk of back to back promotions. The ridiculous new habit of producing league tables from the first day of the season couldn't even put Millwall in the automatic promotion places. Despite their stunning win, Bradford had matched it against Barnsley and Gillingham had gone one better, beating Preston 5-0 to top the most pointless league table of the season.

If that wasn't enough to bring McGhee's men and Millwall's fans down to earth, the half time score in their first away league match at Birmingham certainly was.

After a steady opening twenty minutes at St Andrews

the home side ran amok, scoring four without reply before the break. The match finished 0-4 and Millwall had the odd opening week record of having played two, won one, scored four and conceded four.

A 2-1 League Cup home win over Cardiff with goals from Sadlier and Claridge was slightly more encouraging. But there were worrying signs that Millwall may not yet be quite up to the challenge of the higher level with meek defeats at home to Burnley (0-2) and away to Crewe (0-1). Lions fans travelled to the long-awaited London derby at Crystal Palace with just a single win in their opening four league matches and fearing a humiliation at Selhurst.

They needn't have worried.

Daydreams & Nightmares - Millwall FC in the 2000s - Part 1

9. Palace, Palace, who the...

September 2001...
1 September – Football commentator Brian Moore dies aged 69; 11 September – Approximately 2,977 victims are killed or fatally injured in attacks at the World Trade Center in New York City, The Pentagon, and in Pennsylvania after American Airlines Flight 11 and United Airlines Flight 175 are hijacked and crash into the World Trade Center's Twin Towers, American Airlines Flight 77 is hijacked and crashes into the Pentagon, and United Airlines Flight 93 is hijacked and crashes into grassland in Shanksville, as a result of passengers fighting to regain control of the airplane. The World Trade Center towers collapse as a result of the crashes. 67 UK nationals perish, the largest loss of life from any nation other than the United States; 13 September – Iain Duncan Smith becomes leader of the Conservative Party after winning the leadership election.

In a thrilling derby that would have certainly met the approval of the late ITV commentator Brian Moore, who had sadly passed away the week before, the first half at Palace ended with two goals in sixty seconds.

Richard Sadlier struck first, but before the celebrations of the Millwall fans had died down, Clinton Morrison struck the equaliser right on the half time whistle.

The expected Palace comeback did not materialise and Millwall went straight for their opponents again from the restart, with ex-Eagles striker Claridge getting his third of the season within two minutes. Rather than suffer an onslaught from the home side, Millwall comfortably kept their neighbours at arms length, their fans enjoying the occasion with regular choruses of their own version of the Roy Chubby Brown hit from the previous year.

The x-rated stand-up had recorded a speakover version of the Smokey Hit *Living Next Door To Alice*, in which he led the chant of: *"Alice? Alice? Who the f**k is Alice?"* after each chorus.

It wasn't a great leap for Lions fans to replace "Alice" with "Palace", and the chant filled the air intermittently with the standards 'monks chant' and *No-one Likes Us* as Millwall enjoyed possibly one of their most comfortable wins at Selhurst Park in recent memory. Sadlier and Claridge tormented the Palace defence and the goal threat of Morrison was easily snuffed out by a Lions backline that was, to the relief of McGhee and the travelling fans, in top form. It could and really should have been much more than 2-1 going into injury time.

The chants turned to cheers in the final minute as Claridge capitalised on a real howler from Palace defender Popovitch who managed to head the ball past his own onrushing 'keeper under pressure from Claridge on the edge of the area.

The result was Claridge's fourth goal of the season just needed to be rolled into an empty net in front of Millwall's delirious fans.

The match also saw the one and only appearance of Phil Stamp for The Lions. The central midfielder had made a name for himself at his native Middlesbrough as a tough enforcer, but after a ten year spell that saw him star for 'Boro in Premier League matches and an FA Cup final, had struggled with injuries.

McGhee brought him in on loan and he was being touted as a 'Terry Hurlock-type character' which is always a dangerous thing to do. As he ambled awkwardly on to the Selhurst Park pitch on 67 minutes it was abundantly clear to every fan in the stadium that he was far from match fit. That was a far kinder description than was afforded him by the fans in the away end who discussed amongst themselves the many ways that he was *not* like Terry Hurlock. He spent the last 20 minutes of the match as a virtual spectator and returned to Teesside shortly after, moving to Scottish Premier League side Hearts a year later where he enjoyed three seasons and became something of a cult hero with the Edinburgh club's fans.

If Millwall fans hoped this was some sort of watershed for their wobbly start to the season they were soon disappointed. Division One life came at you fast and, after being dumped out of the League Cup at Gillingham four days after the joy of victory at Palace, they slumped to a numbing 0-1 loss at the same Preston side who The Gills had thumped 5-0 just weeks earlier.

Obviously Millwall were still finding their feet at this level and inconsistency was nothing new - even in their charge to the title the season before - but it did feel like defences at this level were able to tame The Lions' various goal threats far easier than their Division Two opponents.

One of those goal threats was of course missing. But as Millwall fans arrived at The Den to hear the team news for the next match at home to Barnsley, they were dismayed to hear his name once more.

The buzz that reverberated around the stadium when it was announced that Neil Harris had been named as one of the substitutes was up there with the rumour that Birmingham were losing at Sheffield Wednesday on that fateful day in 1972 that Millwall thought they had finally won promotion to the top flight. Only this one was real.

Even a Bruce Dyer opener for the Yorkshire side that sent Millwall in at half time 0-1 down couldn't dampen the spirits of the home fans who were anticipating a second half fairytale. The introduction of winger Christophe Kinet on 56 minutes had an immediate effect, the Belgian wideman crossing for Claridge to level the scores and the cheers turned to roars two minutes later when fans saw Harris stripping off ready to come on.

The welcome that greeted his return would have been enough to put a lump in the throat of even the most hard-faced docker and the momentum that the talismanic Harris gave his side soon paid off.

Claridge struck his sixth goal in ten league and cup matches ten minutes after Harris' introduction and Cahill sealed a fine 3-1 that looked highly improbably at the start of the half. All it lacked was a Harris goal, but unfortunately, that part of the fairytale would be delayed.

Millwall were able to do what they hadn't managed so far that season and back up a win with a string of unbeaten matches. Sheffield United were the latest Yorkshire side to leave SE16 pointless four days later with Nethercott and Kinet on target in a 2-0 win and encouraging draws at Wimbledon (2-2) and Walsall (0-0) set The Lions up nicely for the televised trip to promotion hopefuls West Brom.

Televised football had entered a new era at the start of the 2001-2002 season. ITV had launched their ITV Sport channel - a subscription service that bought the rights to the English Football League. The share of the pot put up by the new channel for Division One clubs was so hugely disproportionate to the other two divisions, it meant that failure to gain promotion from Division Two in 2001 could have seen clubs drift apart from what would become their far wealthier Division One rivals.

Millwall chairman Theo Paphitis made no secret of how vital it was that the club be part of this higher echelon of the TV share, but right from the off, there were rumblings that all might not be going to plan for the new channel. The ITV Sport cameras were at The Hawthorns to show its modest viewing public the sight of Claridge and Sadlier terrorising the Baggies backline, just as they had done to Palace a month before.

The Irish striker grabbed both goals in a 2-0 win which was sealed before the half hour mark. The cameras also managed to capture a cheeky ex-Birmingham striker Claridge reminding the disgruntled home fans in the Birmingham Road Stand of the score.

After the match, ITV Sport pundit Robbie Earl was in no doubt which of the two sides looked like Premier League promotion hopefuls as Millwall's ascent of the Division One table began to gather pace.

A thrilling 3-3 draw at home to Nottingham Forest saw Millwall concede a first half lead through Cahill to two Stern John goals either side of the hour mark. Paul Ifill appeared to have salvaged a point with an 87th-minute leveller, only for John to seal his hat-trick 60 seconds later.

Fans who had inexplicably left The Den early were seen celebrating in the railway tunnel that linked the stadium to Ilderton Road as Sadlier saved a point in injury time with his third goal in two matches.

Stern John would return to haunt Millwall late in a match before the season was over however...

Harris had made another substitute appearance in that 2-2 draw at Wimbledon but had, with little explanation from the club, disappeared from the subs bench afterwards, to be replaced by the enigmatic Savarese. This sparked rumours that his return had perhaps been made too soon.

Goals continued to flow in his (and Savarese's) absence with Bradford beaten 3-1 at The Den courtesy of goals from Sadlier and Cahill and they saved one of their best away performances in recent years to slay a very poignant ghost. Five years earlier at Edgeley Park, news filtered amongst the few hundred or so hardy souls that had travelled from south London to Stockport on a chilly January afternoon that Millwall Football Club had entered administration. They knew that such a step threatened the very existence of the club.

The crushing 1-5 defeat that followed that day only served to deepen a depression that would hang like a dark cloud over the club for many months.

Stockport went on to win promotion that season. Millwall were just lucky to still be able to play in the third tier the next campaign. Four years of hard work had finally seen The Lions rebuild the club, virtually from scratch and they returned to Stockport a very different team.

Since that day, the Cheshire side had shocked the footballing world by reaching the League Cup semi finals and coming within a few points of clinching a place in the play-offs to gain promotion to the top flight for the first time in their history.

Now however, these two teams were passing each other in opposite directions, at rapidly increasing speeds.

Rooted to the foot of the table, Stockport were completely blown away by a virtuoso first half Millwall performance where every single player found the very top of his form.

County were spectators as first Cahill, then Reid and then Claridge scored before the break as Millwall ambled to half time without breaking sweat. Had they decided to up the gears the half time score could easily have been doubled.

It was damage limitation for Stockport after Claridge netted his second from the spot two minutes after the restart and the game ended 4-0 to Millwall, the spectre of that grey day back in 1997 well and truly exorcised.

Just as Millwall were starting to edge tantalisingly close to those play-off places, travelling to top-of-the-table Wolves in ninth place, it was a familiar face who stalled their charge with Alex Rae scoring a 90th-minute winner for the midlands side ending October on a slightly disappointing note.

The fact that Millwall fans left Molineux aggrieved that they hadn't got anything from a trip to the big-spending league leaders and favourites for promotion to get them closer to the Division One play-off places spoke volumes of how far the club had come in such a short time.

It was only to be a temporary setback however. Back to back wins at The Den against Coventry and Rotherham followed by more late drama in a 2-2 draw at Grimsby to send Millwall into those precious top six places had dreams of a return to the big time taking shape:

Nationwide League Division 1 - Nov 24th 2001						
	P	W	D	L	F	A	PTS
1. Burnley	20	11	4	5	39	28	37
2. Wolves	18	10	5	3	28	14	35
3. Crystal Palace	18	11	1	6	41	26	34
4. Norwich	20	10	3	7	27	26	33
5. Preston	20	8	8	4	33	24	32
6. MILLWALL	**19**	**9**	**5**	**5**	**34**	**23**	**32**

Coventry, who were playing their first season outside the top flight since 1967, were desperate for an immediate return and arrived at The Den on a rich run of form that had propelled them to second place. The prolific Jay Bothroyd cancelled out Claridge's first half opener to make it 2-1 after a Warner own goal had levelled six minutes before and, with less than ten minutes remaining, The Sky Blues appeared to be leaving south London with all three points.

Christophe Kinet was proving something of an enigma with some Millwall fans believing him to be a luxury player that did not offer the side enough when starting. But he proved invaluable off the bench when he came on as a sub for full back Ronnie Bull and scored an 81st-minute equaliser. The comeback was complete when Sadlier scored a last-minute winner to seal a brilliant 3-2 win.

A single Cahill goal was enough to see off Rotherham in the next home win and there was more late drama at Grimsby as Millwall fell 1-2 behind in the 88th minute only for Claridge to save a point. Millwall were flying.

As is often the case though, especially at Millwall, the footballing fates conspire to kick you right between the legs, just when you think you're on your way.

When Tim Cahill gave Millwall the lead at home to Gillingham with 20 minutes left, Lions fans were checking scores elsewhere to see just how close their team had now made it to the Division One summit. They didn't just want a shot at promotion back to the top flight for the first time in over ten years through the play-offs. They wanted to do it in style, just as they had done in 1988, by winning the league.

By the time Mr Brandwood placed his whistle to his lips to end the match, it was the fans in the away end at The Den that were celebrating. Goals from Ipoua and King in the final seven minutes had deprived Millwall of a fourth consecutive home win and dumped them back into eighth place.

Such is the competitiveness of English football's second tier, teams were building momentum for a promotion push all around Millwall. So much so that, even though The Lions were able to return quickly to winning ways with a

2-1 win at Bradford, Millwall found themselves dropping two places to tenth before the visit of out-and-out title favourites Manchester City.

The Valley Parade victory had seen late drama for the fifth match in the club's last six matches with home striker Blake equalising in the 90th minute only for Sean Dyche to head a dramatic last gasp winner. The much-anticipated match against Kevin Keegan's Manchester City allowed Millwall what they hoped would be a slight advantage.

Following crowd trouble when the two teams met previously two seasons before, visiting fans were banned from the fixture and a raucous 13,000 Lions supporters hoped to see their side halt City's charge towards the top of the table.

The Blues' talismanic striker Shaun Goater gave his side a 23rd-minute lead but this was cancelled out on the stroke of half time by Richard Sadlier.

Ex Lion loan star Darren Huckerby restored the lead in the 68th minute but a Claridge spot-kick two minutes later levelled a pulsating match at 2-2. City's star-studded side proved too much for a Millwall side pushing for a winner however when a Shaun Wright-Phillips goal ten minutes from time settled the match.

The build-up to the match had seen chairman Theo quash some rumours that had been circulating about Millwall's pursuit of a star-studded striker of their own. Talk of The Lions signing Stan Collymore were dismissed by Paphitis as just that.

It certainly would have been an interesting acquisition given the relationship between that particular player and the club down the years, but we would never know...

Far better news was that Neil Harris was again on his way back, the club and player admitting they had needed some more rehabilitation time after his brief reappearance earlier in the season. His latest return would provide a truly iconic moment in the history of the club.

A 1-1 draw away to struggling Sheffield Wednesday came courtesy of The Lions 'keeper and yet more last minute goalscoring exploits. Warner saved a first half Owls' penalty and Sadlier provided the last minute point-saving goal.

McGhee was keen to use his programme notes for the next match at home to Portsmouth to reassure fans he was on the lookout for new faces to strengthen his squad and even admitted receiving letters from fans asking him to go public with the names of his targets! It's almost as if they didn't believe him...

This was probably with good reason to be fair. The ultra-cynical Lions followers believed they could smell bullshit from a mile off and were less than convinced by McGhee's assertions earlier in the season that his attempts to sign new players was being delayed by their targets' involvement in the UEFA Cup. So far all they'd seen was Giovani Savarese and Phil Stamp.

There had been rumours the previous season of Millwall pursuing a midfield target in the shape of Stoke's Graham Kavanagh - who eventually left for Cardiff for a £1m fee that was clearly out of Millwall's budget. Now speculation had started to spread that they were keen on young Manchester City central player Dickson Etuhu.

Loyal midfielder David Livermore had seemingly become the latest fans' scapegoat - in fairness mostly in the relative tiny world of its online presence - and there appeared to be a clamour to replace him with a more dynamic attacking player.

That was not only unfair, but probably unwise. Millwall already had plenty of dynamism in the shape of Tim Cahill and it was Livermore's hugely underrated workrate that allowed Cahill the freedom he enjoyed. The addition of Etuhu could well have severely disrupted the equilibrium of the side. Although fate would deprive them of Cahill soon enough, which may have made a new signing of the Manchester City star's ilk priceless.

Millwall marked the halfway mark of the season with a Thursday night ITV Sport televised win over Pompey, thanks once again to a Sadlier goal. It meant that transfer speculation wasn't just involving players coming into The Den. Premier League heads were being turned by Sadlier's meteoric rise and prolific form, his hold-up play belied his still young years.

Going into 2002, Millwall's fight wouldn't just be to try and bring in new faces and push on for a promotion place. They would struggle to hold on to the young stars that had got them to the very brink of The Premier League.

Admiring glances were also being shot at Cahill, Reid and Ifill and with Lucas Neill being snapped up by Blackburn Rovers, fans started to fear that the exodus may be just around the corner if promotion wasn't achieved that season Sadly, a totally different set of circumstances would go on to deprive them of Sadlier.

A memorable year was rounded off by an impressive 0-0 draw at second-placed Burnley that was in stark contrast to the meek submission at The Den at the start of the season, and topped off perfectly with a 3-0 home thrashing of Crystal Palace on Boxing Day to complete an emphatic double over their rivals. Claridge and Sadlier (2) scoring all of the goals within ten minutes of the second half starting.

Goals from Cahill and Reid to end 2001 with a 2-0 home win over Crewe was symbolic of the reason Millwall would go into the new year in the top six and vying for a place in the Premier League.

Years of hard work and investment behind the scenes had

produced the best crop of young players fans had seen in decades. Now they were perfectly placed to propel The Lions into the big time:

Nationwide League Division 1 - Dec 31st 2001

	P	W	D	L	F	A	PTS
1. Man City	27	16	4	7	63	36	52
2. Burnley	26	15	5	6	49	38	50
3. Wolves	27	14	7	6	40	23	49
4. Norwich	28	15	4	9	41	36	49
5. MILLWALL	**27**	**14**	**6**	**7**	**48**	**29**	**48**
6. West Brom	28	14	5	9	33	23	47

10. Insult & injury

January 2002...
1 January - Ford unveils their all-new Fiesta supermini which is due on sale in March, but the new model will not be produced in Dagenham, instead, it will be produced in Ford's other European plants in Germany and Spain; 14 January - The foot and mouth crisis is declared over after eleven months; Daniel Bedingfield has a number one hit with Gotta Get Thru This with a record low sales figure of just 25,000 copies...

The new year started for Millwall at Vicarage Road Watford where The Lions were looking to make it four wins out of five and cement their place in the top six. The away end hangovers being nursed from the previous night's revelries were soon forgotten when goals from Cahill and Sadlier either side of the break put Millwall in charge. Reid added a third on 69 minutes and when Heider Helguson scored nothing more than a consolation for the home side in the 82nd minute, the visiting fans were ready to head back around the M25 for home. But Mark McGhee had other ideas.

As the game went into its final minutes, the Millwall manager summoned Harris. The striker had made a much more encouraging return to first team action than his abruptly-ended stint at the start of the season and this was his sixth consecutive appearance, four coming as sub with starts in the previous two home wins over Palace and Crewe.

McGhee told Harris to go on, get a few more minutes under his belt, keep the ball in the corner, and get a goal.

And that's what he did. Every single Millwall fan alive knew that whenever Harris' comeback goal came it would be greeted with the biggest celebration supporters and players at the club had ever seen for a goal. But even they couldn't have been prepared for the goal - and response that was about to unfold.

Harris gathered the ball in the middle of the pitch just inside his own half and, after evading a Watford challenge, set off into the home side's territory - towards the corner as instructed.

But then, as Harris' run took him to the edge of the Watford 18 yard box, he decided on a change of plan. He cut inside and before the Hornets' defenders could do anything about it, unleashed an unstoppable curling shot into the right hand corner of the net.

Cue pandemonium.

Harris headed towards the delirious travelling fans, arms triumphantly aloft and was soon joined by all ten of his teammates who held him aloft in what would go down as one of the most iconic moments and images in football.

Harris' inspirational comeback was complete, he was back and now there seemed to be nothing stopping this Millwall side from storming into the Premier League.

The Boxing Day win over Palace had seen a collection for The Cancer Research Institute. The generosity of both sets of fans in raising almost £4,200 was matched by that of the Palace chairman Simon Jordan who doubled the figure.

The visit of Scunthorpe for Millwall's first FA Cup third round tie in six years was suddenly seen as something of an unwelcome distraction. It was the middle match of a run of five home games in six. The next two league encounters against Birmingham and Watford were seen as perfect opportunities to collect maximum points ahead of trips to promotion rivals Norwich and league leaders Manchester City and end the month vying for a place in the top two.

A routine 2-1 win over Scunthorpe thanks to two more goals from Sadlier provided the taster for revenge over Birmingham who had inflicted Millwall's biggest loss of the season way back in August on their first away league game.

The Lions went into the game nestled nicely in fifth place, four points off top-of-the table Manchester City and two clear of seventh-placed Birmingham, but without Sadlier.

The striker had sustained a knock, frustratingly in the FA Cup match that Millwall could have easily done without, and joined Paul Ifill and Christophe Kinet on an injury list that was starting to give cause for concern.

Ifill had bruised the bones on the top of his foot two months before but decided to play through the pain barrier, which proved insurmountable after his sub appearance against Palace on Boxing Day.

He was now having treatment and, thanks to the restorative qualities of Beckenham Baths, swimming his way back, he hoped, to first team action.

Without the creativity of Ifill and the presence of Sadlier, Millwall struggled to impose themselves on a tough Birmingham side who took the lead on the stroke of half time through Mooney.

Fortunately Dyche was able to grab the equaliser in the second half but there was no way through the Brum defence and Millwall had to be content with a point after winning five of their last six. It meant that, with Watford to visit five days later, The Lions were still in the top six.

The match was marred when, after a string of poor decisions by the assistant referee, a pie was hurled in his direction. The predictable media hysteria followed, with calls for the ground to be shut down and ludicrous questions asked along the lines of: "*It may have only been a pie this time, but next time it could be...*" followed by suggestions ranging from a machete to a molotov cocktail. The story even managed to travel to the opposite side of the world with The New Zealand Herald picking up on it.

The pie was actually followed by a few plastic bottles and cigarette lighters (after the stadium announcer warned the game could be called off - with Millwall 0-1 down maybe that was seen as a goo move) but it was the £2.30 Ginsters delicacy that the press seemed obsessed with.

Three years earlier, in an FA Cup tie between Oldham and Chelsea at Boundary Park, a hot dog was lobbed onto the pitch by disgruntled home fans. It hit referee Paul Durkin who was comically attended to by St John Ambulance staff who one can only assume were well trained in the treatment of Frankfurter abrasions.

The press, whilst dutifully relaying that Durkin would report the matter to the FA and the club faced the possibility of a fine, made light of the issue in a way they would never entertain if the exact same incident had occurred at The Den. Of course this doesn't make the incident against Birmingham right, but the difference in media reaction is there for all to see.

Sadlier was again absent for the home match against Watford but Ifill made a welcome return off the bench. Fortunately, despite another lack lustre Lions attacking display, a 1-0 win was secured courtesy of a Claridge penalty on the half hour to take Millwall, for the time being at least, into the automatic promotion places:

Nationwide League Division 1 - Jan 16th 2002						
	P	W	D	L	F	A	PTS
1. Man City	28	17	4	7	66	37	55
2. MILLWALL	**29**	**15**	**7**	**7**	**50**	**30**	**52**
3. Wolves	28	15	7	6	43	24	52
3. Burnley	27	15	6	6	49	38	51
4. Norwich	29	15	4	10	42	39	49
6. West Brom	29	14	6	9	33	23	48

The point from the goalless draw at Norwich was seen very much as one gained, especially with Sadlier still missing and Ifill only ready to make another second half cameo off the bench. The winger did make a start in the next home match which saw Millwall exit the FA Cup at the fourth round stage to Premier League Blackburn thanks to a late Andy Cole goal. Few tears were shed over the end of The Lions' FA Cup campaign, with thoughts very much on the next trip to the north west.

News that Sadlier would be able to start the crucial top-of-the-table clash at Manchester City was encouraging as The Lions would need to be at their best to have any chance of taking a similarly valuable point home from Maine Road.

Behind the scenes, there were growing concerns over Sadlier's fitness. McGhee had moved to secure some back up in the shape of striker Richard Naylor on loan from Premier League Ipswich. He went straight into the starting lineup for the rested Harris and formed what McGhee hoped would be the sort of robust front two alongside Sadlier that would give the City defence something to think about.

Millwall's stubborn resilience lasted almost 80 minutes - thanks largely to a first half penalty save by Warner - until it was broken, inevitably, by Shaun Goater. The Bermudan settled the match with his second three minutes from time to leave Lions fans thoroughly sick of the sight of him.

City were starting to accelerate ahead at the top of the

division now, leaving just one automatic place to fight for. It was hardly surprising. Keegan had assembled his side at a cost of £12m, McGhee's Millwall cost £750,000.

The fact that two decades on from that financial mismatch, £12m probably wouldn't buy you a striker capable of getting the goals to win promotion to the Premier League, while City spend almost £2bn on league domination speaks volumes of how far the game has gone.

Back at The Den, Sadlier and Harris rolled back the years with a goal apiece, but it was to prove a frustrating afternoon against Walsall with the midlands side cancelling out Sadlier's opener and taking the lead with an 80th minute penalty. Fortunately a Harris spot kick three minutes later earned Millwall their third draw in five matches, but with only one of those being won, Millwall's march on the top two had been halted and The Lions slipped down to fourth.

First half goals from Ifill and Cahill got February off to a flying start with a 2-1 win away to Nottingham Forest and another Cahill goal settled a tight encounter with third placed West Brom at The Den ten days later to see The Lions leapfrog The Baggies into third place.

It was a third place that Millwall would hold on to following the next home game - but only by luck. Wimbledon had often proved a bogey side for The Lions and despite The Dons being in the descendancy since their relegation from The Premier League and various behind-the-scenes shenanigans, the mid-table side managed to nick a 1-0 win from SE16 and inflict Millwall's first home defeat in two months.

Another player returning from injury was on target at Barnsley. Christophe Kinet giving his side the lead in the first half at Oakwell which was cancelled out by Lumsden for another draw.

It was to prove a false dawn in terms of McGhee having a

full squad to choose from however as the season approached its crucial run-in period.

Steve Claridge, himself returning from a knock, scored two goals as Millwall eased aside Preston at The Den 2-1. But in the 21st minute, Sadlier had to be substituted. Fans assumed the change was a precaution and, after treatment for his latest knock the striker would be back in the Lions' starting eleven. The truth was very different. Behind the scenes, the seriousness of Sadlier's injury quickly became apparent, meanwhile on the pitch, Millwall's season threatened to unravel.

Bottom-placed Stockport were beaten 3-0 at The Den in the last game of March, but the weeks leading up to what would prove to be a first victory in five attempts were nothing short of disastrous.

First Millwall travelled to struggling Portsmouth, yet found themselves inexplicably 0-2 down within ten minutes. The shellshocked Lions couldn't recover and ended up losing 0-3.

Then the city of Sheffield conspired to hammer more nails into Millwall's automatic promotion coffin. First Wednesday arrived at The Den down in 19th place with just one win in their previous five matches. McGhee had secured another loan signing in the shape of Irish midfielder Stephen McPhail. It was a puzzling move for Lions fans who felt their midfield was well stocked. The loan spell of Naylor had been cut short with the red-haired striker not providing suitable striking cover and with Sadlier out this was now surely the position that needed addressing.

McGhee attempted to shuffle his pack, playing Ifill up front with Claridge and new boy McPhail plugging the midfield gap. To say it was a disastrous debut was the understatement of the season.

Two goals in a minute from Wednesday's Donnelly settled

the match with fifteen minutes remaining and it descended into farce six minutes later when McPhail was dismissed by referee Paul Alcock. Seconds after play resumed, Dyche nicked a goal but Millwall's blunt attack could not find an equaliser.

Three days later at Bramall Lane there was even more late drama. An initially uneventful match seemed to be heading for a much-needed three points for the travelling Lions. Ifill had given them a first half lead, which was cancelled out by Tonge in the 67th minute but Stuart Nethercott had restored the advantage six minutes later and his defence seemed to holding firm as the match slipped into its final minutes.

By the time the final whistle blew, Millwall fans staggered into the chilly south Yorkshire air bewildered by what they had witnessed. Two goals from Blades' striker Peter Ndlovu in the final two minutes of the match had snatched victory away from them, the 2-3 defeat sending them down to sixth. Worse was to follow at Gillingham days later when the Kent side strolled to a 1-0 win to complete the double over Millwall where a red card for Kinet compounded their misery.

As the transfer window closed days before that victory over Stockport, Mark McGhee hoped that he had pulled off a similarly successful coup to the one that had seen him secure the services of Steve Claridge twelve months before. Dion Dublin arrived on loan from Aston Villa, marking his Lions' debut with the 12th-minute opener in the 3-0 win. In markedly similar circumstances to Claridge's arrival, the powerful frontman arrived at the club at a time when their promotion chances appeared to be slipping away and a big recovery was needed in the final four matches going into April.

11. Here we go again...

April 2002...
9 April - The funeral of Queen Elizabeth The Queen Mother takes place at Westminster Abbey, London. The burial takes place at St. George's Chapel, Windsor; 25 April - Two 16-year-old twin brothers are cleared of murdering 10-year-old Damilola Taylor, who was stabbed to death in South London 17 months earlier; The UK music charts are dominated by reality show Popstars with winner Will Young's March number one being replaced by runner up Gareth Gates in April...

As was the case two seasons before, a torrid spell just ahead of the crucial run-in had seen Millwall drop from top two hopefuls to clinging on to a play-off place for dear life. That wobble was ridden out when it threatened to reappear the previous season, thanks to the acquisition of Claridge. Now, with a tricky run-in of four games that included matches against second placed Wolves and fifth placed Coventry, Birmingham were snapping at The Lions' heels, behind them by virtue of just one goal - and with a game in hand.

Millwall desperately needed to start the month with maximum points going into the home match with Wolves and a trip to Rotherham seemed the perfect way to do it.

The Millers seemed to be slipping back into Division Two and were without a win in six. With Richard Sadlier back in the starting line-up alongside Dublin, McGhee hoped he could out-muscle robust Rotherham. But Sadlier exited the match in the 68th minute and The Lions left with just a point in a goalless draw. Fortunately, other teams around them were also starting to wobble. Burnley's 1-1 draw at Portsmouth on the same day was their fourth without a win and Coventry were embarking on a run that would see them win just two of their last eleven matches. Suddenly Millwall were in fifth place again.

The arrival of second-placed Wolves five days later saw one of the most raucous atmospheres experienced since the Lions' new stadium opened almost a decade before.

The midlands club had catapulted into automatic promotion contention with seven consecutive wins during February and March but arrived at SE16 looking vulnerable with just one win in their last six.

In a match that was tourniquet-tight and certain to be settled by a single incident, Steve Claridge showed all of his experience and composure to despatch a 71st minute penalty and win the game, moving Millwall up to fourth ahead of the trip to Coventry.

By the time Millwall arrived at Highfield Road, results elsewhere had pushed The Lions back down into sixth but the Sky Blues had by now plummeted to tenth.

For once, Millwall were playing a rival at the right time and the 1-0 victory secured by another Claridge goal flattered the hosts.

Dublin had indeed proved a brilliant addition. Claridge was revitalised, clearly enjoying the foil that the big front man provided - which he had badly missed in the absence of Sadlier. Now, with just one match remaining, all Millwall needed was to end the season with victory against Grimsby to secure a place in the play-offs and a chance to reach the Premier League.

Before the match, Millwall announced their Supporters' Player of The Season. The choice was never really in any doubt. Since his arrival, Steve Claridge had given absolutely everything in every minute he'd worn the Millwall shirt. They appeared to be a match made in heaven. He had endured some injuries that, at the time, had fans fearing he had played his last game for the club, and yet in typical Claridge style had come back fighting and, it seemed, stronger than ever.

His award was preceded by a montage of his goals from the season on the stadium scoreboard, to a backdrop of Bowie's *Heroes*. It was a classy touch, a true goosebumps moment going into one of the biggest weeks of the club's history.

Claridge started the match on the bench, McGhee wisely saving his talismanic 17-goal striker after a hectic previous two matches but he came on to rapturous applause when he replaced Dublin on the stroke of half time.

By then, the play-off place was assured. A sixth-minute goal from Dublin and an encouraging double from the ever-improving Harris giving Millwall a 3-1 half time lead that would prove to be the final score. All that was left now was to find out who their play-off opponents would be.

Fourth place had been secured, meaning home advantage in the second leg. That of course had not helped them in their previous two play-off quests for a top flight place when first match defeats at Brighton and Derby rendered The Den tie meaningless.

As expected, Manchester City had won the title at a canter with 99 points. Almost unbelievably for Millwall fans however was, ten points behind them, West Brom had secured the runners up spot and final automatic promotion place. The Baggies had proved to be one of Millwall's easiest opponents that season and only pipped midland rivals Wolves to second place by three points. The Hawthorns side would have proved to be a very palatable play-off opponent, although as we know, league results mean nothing in the end of season lottery. Wolves had faded badly and finished third. They would face Norwich who had sneaked into the top six by the tightest of margins over Burnley. Both teams ending the season on 75 points with Norwich securing the final play-off berth by virtue of a +9 goal difference - one better than The Clarets.

Birmingham had finished their season strongly. With just two defeats in their last fifteen games, they were the dreaded '*team with momentum*' that nobody fancied facing in the play-offs. They would play Millwall.

The tension was palpable as the two teams kicked off for the first leg at St Andrews a week after the season's end. McGhee's message will have been simple: no repeats of the league match here!

Going in at half time, Millwall would have been the happier, but when Bryan Hughes put the home side ahead - despite protests of offside - within seven minutes of the restart, the huge band of travelling Lions fans must have been fearing the worst.

But Millwall managed to first contain, and then frustrate Birmingham, who clearly felt 1-0 was not enough to take to The Den.

With ten minutes left and Birmingham's threat of more goals seemingly snuffed out, Millwall would have been happy to take just the single goal deficit to The Den. But it was about to get better than that...

A ball out wide to Reid was whipped in to the edge of the six yard box and there was the on-loan Villa man Dion Dublin to head home and sicken the home fans with the equaliser and level the two-legged tie at its half time.

Millwall, it was felt, were almost there.

Four days later a white-hot Den welcomed their team onto the pitch in what they hoped would be the start of an historic few weeks for The Lions. Victory would see them face Wolves or Norwich in the Wembley final, with a place in the top flight at stake. Confidence in the build-up was shaken when Birmingham decided to go for Millwall's throats from the off and after sustained pressure, The Lions had young full back Ronnie Bull to thank for chesting a Brum strike to safety after the shot seemed goalbound.

Gradually Millwall grew into the game and, in first half injury time, it looked like they had the breakthrough.

A Reid corner was flapped at by Brum stopper Vaesen and the ball looped tantalisingly toward the visitors' goal. Waiting, almost on the goal line, was Tim Cahill. All he had to do it seemed was nod the ball over the line.

Millwall fans had seen the Australian midfielder rise and hang in the air to score countless goals with his head in the last few seasons. On this occasion however, he was probably too close and was unable to steer his header into the net. Instead it clipped the Birmingham bar and bounced to safety.

Sensing a winner, Millwall pressed on in the second half and another Vaesen howler seemed certain to give The Lions the advantage. He fumbled a cross and it landed at Dion Dublin's feet just outside the six yard box. With the goal at his mercy, the usually ruthless striker must have been so shocked to have suddenly been presented with this gilt-edged chance to win the match that his first time shot lacked the composure that he usually displayed and it drifted agonisingly wide of the grateful Vaesen's far post.

Sensing luck was on their side, Birmingham went in search of a goal to win the tie for themselves. As Millwall poured forward, the visitors cleared their lines following another Lions onslaught and, to the horror of most of the capacity crowd, the clearance found striker Stern John away with only Warner to beat.

As Millwall fans held their breath, expecting to see the net bulge, the Trinidadian who had been signed from Nottingham Forest during the transfer window, had a rush of blood to the head and skied his chance.

The home fans responded with a mixture of relief and mirth. Remembering the fact that the frontman had tormented The Lions with a hat-trick in his previous visit with Forest, they mocked the miss as John stood, alone in the centre of the Millwall half, bewildered at his wayward strike. But it wasn't his last involvement in the match.

Worryingly Birmingham were now becoming the dominant side, attacking with pace down both flanks. Moody and Vickers were keeping the Millwall defence busy and Stern John looked keen to atone for his miss.

The 90 minutes ebbed away as both teams looked to the pre-extra time break to regroup but Claridge almost scored against his old employer with a looping shot reminiscent of his goal against Rotherham the previous season, but it failed to dip enough and sailed inches over the bar.

Then Birmingham came back at Millwall, the ever-dangerous Horsfield also coming just inches from a goal.

With minutes left before the tie went to extra time, Stern John had the opportunity to make up for his earlier miss when he managed to make himself enough space to shoot from the edge of the Lions' area with a clear sight on Warner's goal. But the shot was again off target and the clock ticked down, with surely just enough time for a Birmingham corner before referee Laws blew for full time and an extra 30 minutes to try and decide the tie and avoid the dreaded penalties.

The corner was cleared and the anxious crowd awaited the sound of the official's whistle, but it didn't come. The ball was collected by a Birmingham attacker and whipped speculatively into the Lions' area where two Millwall players looked to clear the danger but only succeeded in getting in each other's way and deflecting the ball out wide to the waiting Vickers on the Millwall left.

Moving menacingly into the area, he sent his cross over early, the Millwall defence was woefully out of position and the ball found Stern John waiting on the edge of the six yard box. The striker couldn't believe his luck as he calmly turned the ball into the unguarded Millwall net.

It was all over.

The whistle blew almost immediately and Millwall's players sunk to their knees in despair as Birmingham's delirious fans celebrated wildly in the away end. The home fans were numb. It was impossible to take in.

As Millwall's shellshocked fans showed their appreciation to a team that had, once again come agonisingly close to winning promotion to the top flight but failed in the play-offs, outside something far more sinister than mere footballing failure was manifesting itself.

Missing out on promotion was soon to be the least of Millwall Football Club's troubles.

NATIONWIDE LEAGUE DIVISION ONE
FINAL TABLE 2001/2002

1	**Manchester City**	46	31	6	9	108	52	+56	99
2	**West Brom**	46	27	8	11	61	29	+32	89
3	Wolves	46	25	11	10	76	43	+33	86
4	**MILLWALL**	46	22	11	13	69	48	+21	77
5	**Birmingham City**	46	21	13	12	70	49	+21	76
6	Norwich City	46	22	9	15	60	51	+9	75
7	Burnley	46	21	12	13	70	62	+8	75
8	Preston North End	46	20	12	14	71	59	+12	72
9	Wimbledon	46	18	13	15	63	57	+6	67
10	Crystal Palace	46	20	6	20	70	62	+8	66
11	Coventry City	46	20	6	20	59	53	+6	66
12	Gillingham	46	18	10	18	64	67	-3	64
13	Sheffield United	46	15	15	16	53	54	-1	60
14	Watford	46	16	11	19	62	56	+6	59
15	Bradford City	46	15	10	21	69	76	-7	55
16	Nottingham Forest	46	12	18	16	50	51	-1	54
17	Portsmouth	46	13	14	19	60	72	-12	53
18	Walsall	46	13	12	21	51	71	-20	51
19	Grimsby Town	46	12	14	20	50	72	-22	50
20	Sheffield Wednesday	46	12	14	20	49	71	-22	50
21	Rotherham United	46	10	19	17	52	66	-14	49
22	**Crewe Alexandra**	46	12	13	21	47	76	-29	49
23	**Barnsley**	46	11	15	20	59	86	-27	48
24	**Stockport County**	46	6	8	32	42	102	-60	26

millwall 0
rotherham 6

**hangover
02/03**

Daydreams & Nightmares - Millwall FC in the 2000s - Part 1

12. Damage limitation

August 2002...
4 August – 10-year-old girls Holly Wells and Jessica Chapman go missing in Soham, Cambridgeshire; 21 August – Ian Huntley, detained under the Mental Health Act, is charged with the murders of Holly Wells and Jessica Chapman. His girlfriend Maxine Carr is charged with perverting the course of justice. Both are remanded in custody. [17] Meanwhile, police confirm that the two bodies found at Lakenheath are those of the two girls...

May 2002 proved to be one of Millwall Football Club's greatest nadirs. The fallout from the riot that ensued on the streets of Bermondsey following the last minute defeat to Birmingham was unprecedented for the club. What made the trouble that occurred that night so different from previous incidents such as the Luton FA Cup quarter final in 1985 or the play-off semi-final second leg against Derby at The Den in 1994 is that it occurred well away from the stadium.

So, unlike back in '85 or '94, supporters, players and staff within the confines of the ground were blissfully ignorant of the chaos that was unfolding outside.

Chairman Paphitis, understandably gutted that his club

hadn't managed to make that last step into a final game of the season to try and win promotion into the big time, had composed himself and, after sitting in his boardroom surrounded by solemn faces, decided to buck them up by delivering one of his trademark motivational speeches..

He was rightly proud of the team that had been built on a combination of the club's brilliant new youth system, and shrewd recruitment. There was no doubt that they wouldn't stop here and, just as they hadn't given up after losing to Wigan in the play-offs two years before, they would once more regroup, come back stronger next season and look to go straight up as they had done in 2001.

But before he was able to get into his stride he was interrupted by a fellow director who drew his attention to live breaking news reports on the boardroom's television.

They showed a scene of total carnage being played out on the surrounding streets. Police were being bombarded with all manner of missiles with reports of buses and coaches being attacked and police horses being injured - or even killed - the latter thankfully proving unfounded.

The orgy of violence went on for over an hour, while the Birmingham fans remained locked inside The Den. Millwall supporters who were in the stadium walked away without incident, with the trouble apparently started by fifty people throwing missiles and fireworks approximately 30 minutes after the final whistle had blown, spilling out of the warren of side streets of the estate opposite The Den and South Bermondsey train station.

The aftermath reporting was understandably horrified and covered globally. Paphitis finally arrived home at 4am utterly dejected.

It didn't take much investigating however, in the days that followed, to unearth the truth. As had seemed apparent, with no trouble inside the stadium, the riot had been premeditated by a wide variety of hooligans from all over London - and some from the Midlands. Petrol bombs and other missiles had been stashed behind garden walls well in advance of the match and its outcome was of no relevance whatsoever. Had Millwall won the game, the end result outside would have been the same.

Around twenty perpetrators were prosecuted, some received jail terms. Very few had ever had anything to do with Millwall Football Club. Crucially, no doubt concentrating their efforts on the match itself and the supporters inside the stadium that night, the Police had no intelligence whatsoever of this well planned trouble outside it.

Theo Paphitis had leapt to the defence of Millwall supporters in his five year tenure, but on this occasion, even given the external nature of the incident, he had no defence.

The Metropolitan Police were taking legal advice on whether they could sue Millwall Football Club for the damages they had suffered. Paphitis was summoned to an emergency meeting by Police Deputy Commissioner Ian Blair who threatened to shut the club down by withdrawing its safety certificate.

To his credit, Paphitis still tried to defend his club and supporters, rightly pointing out that the events of that night went beyond Millwall Football Club. Whilst an argument could be made that if Millwall hadn't been playing that night it wouldn't have happened, it had to be asked just how far-reaching the club's scope of responsibility was for the actions of people that hadn't attended their football match or stadium!

That was just the first of many meetings Paphitis had to attend with Police through the summer. Far from formulating a plan with manager McGhee to make tweaks to a squad that had come so agonisingly close to promotion and make sure it went one better next term, Theo had a close season of damage limitation to ensure the club was able to start the new season at all.

Only when Paphitis offered a 'members only' solution for the upcoming campaign did the Police agree to allow the club to continue. It was a move that would enrage fans and be the beginning of the erosion of the previously happy relationship between chairman and supporters. What they couldn't possibly appreciate was the immense pressure Theo had been under by the authorities and the power that they wielded to stop the club from operating at all. It was at them - and the relatively small band of thugs that took part in that riot on May 2nd 2002 that their ire should have been directed at.

The say it never rains but it pours and that May it absolutely hammered down on The Den. As if the riot and its ensuing membership scheme wasn't going to hit the club in the pocket enough, it was announced that the debt-ridden ITV Digital had ceased trading.

It plunged many clubs into turmoil. They had set budgets almost solely on the TV revenue from the new channel and had the rug pulled from them with horrifying consequences. Bradford City, Bury, Nottingham Forest, Watford, Barnsley, Lincoln City and Port Vale filed for administration, fearful that the drastic loss of revenue would put them out of business.

Of all the troubled clubs, Bradford City's situation was the most precarious. The West Yorkshire club had debts of £36million and had failed to meet a deadline for a takeover deal. It seemed inevitable that the Bantams, who had gone into liquidation in 1983, would endure a total collapse and lose their place in the Football League. Their only hope was for the Football League to ignore their financial plight and allow them a place in Division One for the 2002–03 season.

Thanks to Theo Paphitis' shrewdness, Millwall were in no such trouble, but they weren't exactly sitting pretty. Promotion to Division One had been seen as crucial in 2001 in order to scoop the bigger share of the TV money ITV Digital were offering to the Football League's top division. Paphitis had been sensible and hadn't put all his eggs in the ITV Digital basket, but there was no doubt the extra revenue helped with essential team modifications such as the loan signing of Dion Dublin which cost a six-figure loan fee and £20,000 per week wages.

There were slim hopes of signing Dublin on a permanent deal for the following campaign. These had been dashed by the financial fallout from the play-off post-match trouble, now the collapse of ITV Digital was to have implications on the current playing squad too with Paphitis having to be even more frugal than he'd ever anticipated.

The season started in understandably subdued fashion with the 7,000 assembled at The Den for the opener against Rotherham the lowest home league crowd for several seasons. It was just as well.

The meagre crowd were to witness a horror show that a Millwall home crowd hadn't come close to witnessing in thirty years.

Byfield and McIntosh gave Rotherham a 2-0 half time lead against a sluggish Lions side, but there was nothing to suggest the slaughter that was to follow.

Byfield ran in four goals in total, almost all without any resistance from a pedestrian Millwall defence and beleaguered Tony Warner in goal. When he stroked home his fourth - and Rotherham's sixth - there was still over ten minutes left to extend the humiliation.

It was Millwall's worst ever home league defeat. Not just in terms of scoreline, but all round team performance. With the greatest respect to Rotherham, this wasn't the Gazza and

Lineker-inspired Tottenham side that ran out 5-0 victors at The Den in 1990; it wasn't even the slick Second Division Grimsby Town team that inflicted a 6-1 FA Cup third round defeat on Peter Anderson's Third Division Lions side in 1982. At least they managed a goal that day.

Rumour across the various Internet messageboards - of which there were now many who had jumped on the online bandwagon set rolling by House of Fun - speculated about unrest in the dressing room.

Allegedly, the costs involved in the administration of the membership scheme and the huge hole left in the income without ITV Digital's big TV revenue payment for the new season meant that contract enhancements promised to the players who had helped take the club from the third tier to withing touching distance of the Premier League had been reneged. No-one likes to accuse footballers of throwing a match and there was never any evidence to suggest this was the case in the 0-6 loss to Rotherham. Like everything else that was going wrong at the club at the time, Millwall fans just had to accept it and move on.

It would take six games for Millwall to register their first win of the season, a 2-0 win over Grimsby thanks to two goals from the evergreen Steve Claridge.

Up until then, the Rotherham debacle had been followed up with a goalless draw at Watford, a 0-1 defeat at Gillingham and after the first goal of the season was scored by young striker Ben May in the fourth match at home to Ipswich, the newly-relegated Suffolk side were able to salvage a point. A comprehensive 1-3 loss at Sheffield United once again saw all the action happen late. Asaba and Tonge gave The Blades a two goal cushion with ten to go, Ifill made it interesting with a goal in the 89th minute but that man Ndlovu once again popped up in injury time to seal it.

Darren Ward scored his first goal for the club in the 1-0 home win over Brighton to start September with a win but it was back down to earth with a bump when lowly Rushden and Diamonds knocked The Lions out of the League cup on penalties after a 0-0 stalemate.

Ward had been another deadline day signing by McGhee the previous season, using up, as it would turn out, the last of the ITV Digital money. The dashing defender quickly earning the nickname The *Peckham Beckham* after his resemblance to the world-famous winger. It was a big investment by Millwall standards. A reported fee of £500,000 was paid to Watford and his initial introduction to the centre of Millwall's defence appeared, rather unerringly, to make the Lions' backline look a little more vulnerable. But he quickly settled in and was proving to be a key part of the back line.

As was becoming the norm at Millwall, every positive occurrence was cancelled out by a negative one and that victory over Brighton was no exception. Influential midfielder Tim Cahill had been subbed after sustaining an knock and scans revealed a knee injury that would keep the Aussie goalscoring central player for most of the season.

The only positive that could be gleaned from this news was that it would delay Cahill's inevitable departure from the club with Premier League clubs ready to make a move now having to curtail their interest.

Returning to The Den was midfielder Andy Roberts. The former Lions youth product had enjoyed a good career in the top flight with Palace and Wimbledon and was now available, which suited Millwall's new trimmed down recruitment budget. Also arriving was veteran striker Kevin Davies on loan. Neil Harris had started every match so far that season but appeared to be struggling to recapture his true form. Which was of course totally understandable.

Southampton loanee Davies made his debut in a 0-1 defeat at Portsmouth, but got on the scoresheet in his next match, giving The Lions a 2-1 lead at Turf Moor - Ian Moore snatching a late equaliser. His home debut proved to be another Den disaster with Walsall easing to a 3-0 win. Millwall went into the next match away to Coventry with just two wins in eleven league and cup matches and in the relegation places.

Davies was on the scoresheet again, but his goal was sandwiched by two first half Sky Blues strikes as Millwall went into the break 1-2 down.

Their luck seemed to be changing when, five minutes into the second half, Kinet equalised to seemingly seal a useful point and stop the rot against the promotion-chasing Coventry and the away fans were rubbing their eyes as Neil Harris scored his first of the season with five left to win the match 3-2. The match saw a Millwall debut for Dennis Wise. The veteran of Wimbledon's Crazy Gang had been made available by Leicester and, following a tip-off from Ray Wilkins who was a mutual friend of both Wise and Paphitis, the deal was done. In typical fashion, Wise marked his Lions bow with a yellow card but, more significantly for one of the game's winners: a win.

Davies was on target for his third goal in four games to give Millwall the lead when fourth placed Nottingham Forest visited The Den next. But the defensive frailties were in evidence once again as two second half David Johnson goals saw them lose a second consecutive home match and third of the season 1-2. It was Wise's home debut where again he picked up a yellow card.

The team was looking fatigued and in desperate need of new impetus. Young full back Ronnie Bull had been in fine form keeping stalwart Robbie Ryan out of the side but was looking jaded - as was Matt Lawrence in the opposite full back position. Ryan had been reinstated for the Forest match, where Lawrence had been dismissed with a second yellow card in the aftermath of their 85th-minute winner so McGhee's hand had been forced somewhat.

After a 1-1 home draw with Wimbledon where Nethercott scored at both ends, Millwall signed promising young defender Glen Johnson on loan from Chelsea. He made his Millwall bow in the 1-3 defeat at promotion-chasing Norwich and Lions fans got their first chance to see him in The Den clash with Derby.

For once, Millwall started on the front foot and Dennis Wise appeared to have well and truly settled. Involved in everything, it was no surprise when the diminutive midfielder opened his Millwall account with a goal just before half time.

Harris appeared revitalised with the addition of Wise too and with Johnson looking equally adept bursting forward as defending, Millwall put in by far their most impressive performance of the season, Harris justifying The Lions' dominance with two late goals to make it 3-0.

The climb away from the relegation zone continued with a rare victory at Hillsborough, Sheffield Wednesday beaten 1-0 thanks to a Claridge goal and even a 0-2 defeat at Reading couldn't discourage The Lions who then went on a run of three wins in the next four matches with Reid, Ifill, Harris and Wise all on the scoresheet in victories at home to Preston (2-1) Bradford (1-0) away at Stoke (1-0) and a creditable 2-2 draw at home to second placed Leicester.

Confidence was high going into the match at Crystal Palace with The Lions up in tenth place but an unlucky 0-1 defeat was followed by a 1-4 thumping at Leicester. The Lions were clearly missing Glen Johnson who had returned to Chelsea and by the time Millwall travelled to Rotherham for the final match of a tumultuous year, their topsy turvy season had taken another dip with no wins in four after draws with Wolves (1-1) and Gillingham (2-2).

Revenge for the 0-6 reverse at the season's opener was on the minds of the 196 travelling Millwall fans at the last match of the year at Millmoor.

After Steve Claridge made it 3-0 to The Lions in the 58th minute -adding to earlier goals from Harris and Reid - the visiting supporters cheekily chanted "*We want six*" as Millwall went some way to banishing the ghost of that season-opening horror show.

Wise was absent from the Rotherham win after accumulating five yellow cards in his fifteen appearances for the club and whilst his presence wasn't missed too much against a rather unwilling Millers, his experience would certainly have been useful in the opening match of the new year. Millwall completely unravelled against an Ipswich side just one place above them in the table and the 1-4 defeat was the third heavy reverse of the season. These were strange times for Millwall supporters. Having spent the last three seasons looking at the top positions in the table and seeing their team so tough to beat, they were now worryingly scanning the relegation places and wondering which version of their team would turn up for the next match.

The answer when Watford arrived at The Den next - following a 1-1 FA Cup third round draw at Cambridge a week earlier - was the good one.

Claridge had scored the goal in the 1-1 draw at The Abbey Stadium and he was on target again to give his side the lead against The Hornets. Another youth prospect in Peter Sweeney made his second appearance of the season from the bench and marked it with an 89th minute goal to seal an impressive 4-0 win.

Claridge was in fine goalscoring form now and made it

three in three as Cambridge were dumped out of the FA Cup in a 3-2 Den replay to set up a fourth round tie away to Premier League Southampton. It was a tie that ex-Portsmouth man Claridge would be relishing.

He made it five in four with both goals in a 2-0 win at Grimsby and his sixth in five looked like pulling off a cup shock at St Mary's when his 17th-minute goal against Southampton separated the sides as the tie went into injury time.

There was an air of inevitability about the scorer of The Saints' injury time equaliser though. Striker Kevin Davies had returned to his parent club after a successful loan spell at The Den. Chances of making the move permanent were again, thanks to the various new financial constraints on the club, non-existent and he of course returned to haunt Millwall with a goal to force a Den replay.

Daydreams & Nightmares - Millwall FC in the 2000s - Part 1

13. A Sads Ending...

February 2003...
15 February - in London, more than 2,000,000 people demonstrate against the Iraq War, the largest demonstration in UK history; 17 February - the London congestion charge, a fee levied on motorists travelling within designated parts of central London, comes into operation.

A 1-0 home win over third placed Sheffield United had Millwall hoping to creep into the top half of the table for only the second time that season but enforced changes all across McGhee's squad would, at least temporarily, put paid to that.

Millwall gave a good account of themselves in the live televised FA Cup fourth round replay against Southampton and Steven Reid made the Premier League Saints fight all the way when he equalised Oakes' opener.

But the top flight side proved too strong for Millwall and Oakes struck again early in extra time to send The Lions out of the cup - and onto another bad run.

Injuries were playing havoc with McGhee's selection and the trip to Preston saw another new recruit slotting into the back four. Sergei Baltacha Jr was the son of Ukranian international and former Dynamo Kyiv and Ipswich star. His sister Elena was a top-seeded tennis player. By now youngsters Charlie Hearn and Alan Dunne had made first team debuts and whilst it was good to see the club continue to blood their youth, this was clearly a matter of necessity in the absence of being able to spend any serious money in the transfer market.

To put it kindly, the Millwall team selection at this time was scattergun and smacked of desperation.

A last minute Kinet goal in the 1-2 Deepdale defeat would be the last Millwall would register for almost as month as three more defeats swiftly followed at home to play-off chasing Reading (0-2) away to relegation-bound Brighton (0-1) where young prospect Moses Ashikodi created Lions history by becoming the youngest player to appear for the club at just 15 years and 240 days old when he came on as a substitute. The goalless run would culminate in yet another home humiliation.

Harry Redknapp had been installed as Portsmouth manager by mega-rich owner Milan Mandarić and had wasted no time spending to assemble a squad that was racing to the title. Pompey did not have to concern themselves with the loss of the ITV Digital TV revenue.

What was, in all but league position, a Premier League side, Redknapp's Portsmouth took Millwall apart at will from the first whistle. Veteran midfielder Paul Merson pulled the strings, helping the livewire striker Yakubu, ex-Spurs and Blackburn star Tim Sherwood and Bulgarian international Svetoslav Todorov to ease Pompey to a 4-0 half time lead.

Millwall fans were fearing a humiliation even greater than the one Rotherham had inflicted on them.

Fortunately, Redknapp appeared to pity the hapless home side and took Merson off after he had made it 5-0 from the penalty spot. The ex-Arsenal man had tortured Millwall and quite rightly earned a standing ovation from the home supporters as he left the pitch. Merson was visibly surprised by the response, but Redknapp wasn't.

When asked about the gesture - one that is hardly ever afforded to visiting players by The Lions' partisan fans no matter how well they have played - in the post-match press conference, Redknapp simply shrugged saying:

"Well, these are proper football supporters here ain't they?"

It was a glowing testament - especially from a West Ham man.

The match did actually have one positive aspect to take away from. The 54th minute appearance of Richard Sadlier was heartening. But word was circulating about the ongoing injury issues the unlucky Irishman was having and his return was viewed with guarded optimism. This latest crushing defeat sent Millwall down to 16th but a Sadlier goal in the 1-1 draw at home to Burnley next up offered hope that not only could Millwall salvage something from this torturous season, but that their striker was well and truly on his way back.

A first win in seven away to Walsall was swiftly followed by 0-2 reverses away to Wimbledon and at home to Norwich to set up what had now become a relegation showdown between the 17th placed Lions and bottom club Sheffield Wednesday at The Den. The descending doom around the Den was darkened further when it was revealed that Sadlier - who had been withdrawn just before the break at Wimbledon - had suffered a relapse of his recurring hip injury.

Fortunately The Lions were able to easily overcome the doomed Owls and it was clear to most that The Lions didn't really have to concern themselves too much with the drop zone. Although the bitter experience of 1996 was still fresh in most Millwall fans' memories so nothing was being taken for granted.

With Sadlier absent, McGhee once again dipped into the transfer market on deadline day. His options were considerably more limited than in previous seasons and there was only a lukewarm welcome afforded to his latest acquisition.

Mark McCammon was an imposing centre forward who had scored ten goals in 75 appearances for Second Division Brentford. Millwall fans were at a loss to understand how he would solve Millwall's number ten issue, with both Claridge and Harris struggling without the support of a partner to hold up play and allow them opportunities to score.

He may not have had any involvement in Harris' last minute winner away to Bradford in his debut, but his influence certainly seemed to have a positive impact on his home bow - a 3-1 win over Stoke - and he got his first goal for the club in the next match, scoring the winner in a 2-1 victory at Derby to make it three wins in his first three matches.

Coming against teams around them in the table, those three wins ended any nagging doubts about Millwall's second tier status. In fact they travelled to face sixth-placed Wolves up in ninth place, and whilst relegation fears had long since been allayed, there was no chance of a late run for a play-off place. That was cemented by a resounding 0-3 defeat at Molineux. It was the fourth away game of the season that Millwall had to play without the backing of their fans. Many league clubs had exercised the option to ban Lions fans from their stadiums in the aftermath of the play-off riot. Wolves followed Stoke, Leicester and Burnley in the move that would also be imposed in the final away match of the season at Nottingham Forest.

Similarly, on Police advice, away fans from Forest, Leicester, Wolves, Portsmouth and Stoke had not been allowed to The Den.

The sort of season that fans are happy to see the back of was petering out with just the visit of Crystal Palace to provide any real interest.

In what proved to be an unusually entertaining game in a season of heavy defeats and flattering victories, a Harris penalty and goal on the stroke of half time from McCammon cancelled out a 22nd minute Palace opener. A Robbie Ryan own goal just three minutes into the second half levelled the match at 2-2 but the stadium came to life four minutes later when Tim Cahill made his long-awaited return from injury.

In typical Cahill fashion, he scored the crucial third goal to seal a 3-2 win in the 74th minute and leave Millwall's season seemingly end on an unexpected high note.

The addition of McCammon certainly seemed to improve Millwall as a goalscoring force - even when he wasn't on the scoresheet himself - and fans had quickly warmed to the all-action big man up front.

The final away match of the season saw Millwall, still in ninth place, travel to play-off hopefuls Nottingham Forest in sixth and the difference in ambition between the two teams was evident when goals from Jess and Bopp gave the home side a commanding 2-0 lead within twenty minutes.

Nethercott quickly grabbed a goal back and a Cahill goal just after the hour mark made it 2-2 but a David Johnson strike with less than twenty minutes left seemed to have settled the match.

There was an eerie silence that greeted Neil Harris' 87th minute equaliser, with the Millwall fans banned from the City Ground, but it was another welcome point in and end-of-season run that had seen The Lions defeated just once in their last seven games.

They rounded off the season making it one in eight with a routine 2-0 victory over Coventry. It was a match that saw 15-year-old Ashikodi come on as a 16th-minute sub for Mark McCammon (which wouldn't be the first time the two would have an exchange of sorts) and a first goal for another youngster in Tony Craig. The rookie defender who hailed from a Millwall-mad family had made his bow in the Palace win and joyously gave his side the lead over the Sky Blues just after the break. The lead was doubled minutes later and the celebrations that greeted the final whistle defied the gloomy backdrop that the season had been played out against.

On reflection, it had actually been a successful campaign. To finish ninth after suffering some horrible defeats both home and away, contending with a crippling injury list to key players and with the spectre of last season's trouble still hanging over them.

The addition of Wise - who had missed a spell through injury but was now back in the side - and his influence over the many young players that had been blooded during the season provided hope for the next.

The summer of 2003 would bring further inevitable change. The books had to be balanced in the face of the last year's dip in revenue and the knock-on effect that the membership scheme had on that with lower attendances. The average turnout at The Den had dropped almost 5,000 from 13,380 to 8,512. A drop of more than 30% that simply could not be absorbed without consequences.

Whilst the ever-growing band of Premier League admirers had been temporarily fended off after the injury to Tim Cahill, they would be back.

Millwall would have to almost completely reinvent themselves for the 2003/2004 season which would see changes in management, players and, almost completely out of the blue, the creation of club history.

NATIONWIDE LEAGUE DIVISION ONE
FINAL TABLE 2002/2003

1	**Portsmouth**	46	29	11	6	97	45	+52	98
2	**Leicester City**	46	26	14	6	73	40	+33	92
3	Sheffield United	46	23	11	12	72	52	+20	80
4	Reading	46	25	4	17	61	46	+15	79
5	**Wolves**	46	20	16	10	81	44	+37	76
6	Nottingham Forest	46	20	14	12	82	50	+32	74
7	Ipswich Town	46	19	13	14	80	64	+16	70
8	Norwich City	46	19	12	15	60	49	+11	69
9	**MILLWALL**	**46**	**19**	**9**	**18**	**59**	**69**	**−10**	**66**
10	Wimbledon	46	18	11	17	76	73	+3	65
11	Gillingham	46	16	14	16	56	65	−9	62
12	Preston North End	46	16	13	17	68	70	−2	61
13	Watford	46	17	9	20	54	70	−16	60
14	Crystal Palace	46	14	17	15	59	52	+7	59
15	Rotherham United	46	15	14	17	62	62	0	59
16	Burnley	46	15	10	21	65	89	−24	55
17	Walsall	46	15	9	22	57	69	−12	54
18	Derby County	46	15	7	24	55	74	−19	52
19	Bradford City	46	14	10	22	51	73	−22	52
20	Coventry City	46	12	14	20	46	62	−16	50
21	Stoke City	46	12	14	20	45	69	−24	50
22	**Sheffield Wednesday**	**46**	**10**	**16**	**20**	**56**	**73**	**−17**	**46**
23	**Brighton**	**46**	**11**	**12**	**23**	**49**	**67**	**−18**	**45**
24	**Grimsby Town**	**46**	**9**	**12**	**25**	**48**	**85**	**−37**	**39**

Daydreams & Nightmares - Millwall FC in the 2000s - Part 1

a dish best served cold...
03/04

Daydreams & Nightmares - Millwall FC in the 2000s - Part 1

14. Everything's changing

August 2003...
3 August – police use the taser for the first time;
10 August – Brogdale, near Faversham, enters the UK Weather Records for the highest ever recorded temperature of 38.5 °C, a record which holds until July 2019. The 2003 European heat wave makes this Britain's hottest summer for thirteen years...

Millwall's new season began with the worst possible news when it was announced, just hours ahead of The Den opener against Wigan, that former coach Ray Harford had lost his battle with cancer. In his brief spell with the club, Harford had shown his immense skills not just in coaching and player management, but in nurturing the young talent that was emerging in The Lions' first team.

The acceleration with which the likes of Reid, Cahill and Ifill had gone from Second Division players to footballers that would not have looked out of place in the Premier League was down in no small part to the experience and influence of Harford.

That was borne out by the summer transfer activity which had seen the inevitable departure of one of that talented trio. Reid had been courted by top clubs for most of the previous season but Millwall had managed to resist, thanks, in part, to the long term injury to one of the others - Tim Cahill. Under different circumstances, both may well have left the previous campaign. The blow of Reid being snapped up by Blackburn Rovers was softened somewhat by the fact that, lining up for that first match of the season in the club's new kit and sponsor, was Cahill - and Ifill. Both of whom were still attracting top flight interest.

New additions to the squad included giant Belgian striker Bob Peeters and Middlesbrough frontman Noel Whelan which did little to inspire fans lamenting the loss of Reid without a high-profile replacement, but there was some promise in the loan acquisition of Brazilian left-back Juan from Arsenal, the first to appear in a Lions shirt.

It proved to be unfulfilled however, making just two starts more than his name, returning to north London after an unremarkable August.

The other two new recruits did prove encouraging during that first month though...

Millwall were sporting a completely new strip which was all blue with white sleeves and a large white stripe down the side of the shorts. The shirt was a nod to one worn by the promotion-winning team under George Graham back in 1984/85 - and the much less remarkable version sported two seasons later when John Docherty took the helm at The Den.

The sponsor was new too. Theo Paphitis' Ryman stationers - who he had rescued in pretty much the same way as he had done Millwall - were now emblazoned across the shirts.

There was an eyebrow-raising change behind the scenes too when McGhee appointed fellow Scot Archie Knox as his assistant.

Knox was renowned as a tough disciplinarian, something

that had been met with varying degrees of Den success. The aforementioned Graham was known to be strict, but had a much more businesslike way of going about it. Players spoke of the aura that surrounded him which many found so intimidating without him having to utter a word. Contract negotiations would often fall apart before the player had even sat down after being told to enter Graham's office. It seemed to work, partly thanks to the very contrasting assistance of Theo Foley who would often put a comforting arm around a player if he had been bawled out by Graham.

Bruce Rioch arrived at The Den in 1990 with a similar reputation and enjoyed some initial success thanks to a 'good cop, bad cop' scenario that had worked so well for Graham and Foley. But once good cop Steve Harrison left under rather dubious circumstances, it all unravelled for Rioch.

Knox assisted Alex Ferguson during a successful spell at Aberdeen in the early 80s and, after dabbling in management, rejoined Fergie at Manchester United.

A student of the 'hairdryer' school of managing, just as this technique was rapidly becoming outmoded since the arrival of Arsene Wenger at Arsenal, fans weren't sure if his appointment was a positive step - especially given the somewhat volatile nature of certain members of The Lions' squad!

It was one of those very characters that got Millwall's season off to the perfect start against newly-promoted Wigan when Dennis Wise scored a 52nd-minute goal and the lead was doubled by Cahill to seal a very satisfying start - and another win against their old Wembley and play-off foes.

The blow of an early exit in the league cup at home to Oxford was quickly forgotten when Whelan announced his arrival. Scoring the only goal of the game in the fifth minute away to Sunderland, giving Millwall two from two and an early second place in the totally irrelevant August table. Whelan was on target again in his first home league start, grabbing an 89th-minute equaliser in the 1-1 draw with Crewe but a drab goalless draw in the next match away to Stoke saw doubts about Millwall's firepower resurface again ahead of the visit of Crystal Palace.

Bob Peeters had so far failed to impress the ultra-cynical Millwall support who had witnessed the six foot five inch tall striker make two starts so far in those two draws and be subbed after an hour in both. He was dropped to the bench for the visit of early table-toppers Palace, leaving Lions fans pining for the departed Steve Claridge who had moved into management with non-league Weymouth.

Making an encouraging appearance from the subs bench was Richard Sadlier who managed fifteen minutes against Crewe and Stoke. Sadly it was to be another false dawn for the unfortunate frontman - and his final one. Just days later he officially announced his retirement from football.

Peeters was introduced to the match with less than fifteen minutes remaining of a game that looked to be heading for an inevitable 1-0 victory for Millwall's far more ruthless rivals. Any fans in that mindset that drifted away from The Den before the final whistle will have missed Bob Peeters' first Millwall goal. No surprise that it was a header, and coming deep into injury time made it all the sweeter for both player and fans.

Fans' disappointment in the club's apparent failure to reinvest the reported (but, as usual, unconfirmed) £3.2m transfer fee received for Steven Reid was understandable. What they can't have appreciated however was the impact of the fallout the season after the Birmingham play-off trouble which cost the club far more in terms of lost revenue. Gates had fallen dramatically, partly due to a poor 2002/03 season, but mostly because of the compulsory membership scheme that Theo Paphitis had been forced to instigate. The fans that felt Paphitis had been cracking a walnut with a sledgehammer were blissfully unaware of the pressure he had been under from the Police and, to his credit, relaxed the compulsory aspect towards the end of the previous season as soon as figures for arrests and incidents at football grounds had been released, showing a marked drop at The Den. The hope was that attendances would once again climb and allow the club to compete in the transfer market once more. But there were other pressing personnel issues.

Key squad members Stuart Nethercott, Dennis Wise Tony Warner, Dave Livermore, Andy Roberts and Matt Lawrence would all be out of contract at the end of the current campaign. Replacing them would be costly, and, fans feared, only financeable by the sale of more stars.

It was a fear enhanced, perversely, by the good news that Paul Ifill had signed a new deal. Supporters felt this was a key tactic in ensuring the best possible fee for the wing wizard, but that was one of football's inescapable facts. Ifill's departure - as that of Cahill - was seen as a matter of "when" rather than "if". They wouldn't have to worry about Wise signing a new playing contract soon though...

Another step in the right direction was the saga of the stadium walkway finally appearing to come to an end. After almost ten years of wrangling, what appeared to most to be a simple matter of providing visiting fans to The Den a way in and out of the stadium without coming into contact with rival supporters was finally rubber-stamped. The plan was to have it completed before the November 1st visit of Nottingham Forest - who had the worst record for football violence the previous season.

There was another key date for the test of Millwall's efforts to prevent the trouble that had caused it so much pain in the last year or so: Saturday March 21st, 2004, when West Ham would visit.

The Lions' bitter rivals had been relegated from the Premier League on the final day of the season, setting up one of the most eagerly-awaited days at The Den for decades.

September began with a trip to Gillingham who were fast becoming The Lions' bogey team. In-form Ifill gave Millwall an early lead but this was wiped out by a Sadibe equaliser on the half hour and the travelling fans' misery was compounded when old boy Paul Shaw sent The Gills in 2-1 up at the break. Referee Keith Hill blew for half time as soon as the players were ready to restart and sent both teams in for half time - even though Shaw's goal had been officially timed at 43 minutes! Hill acknowledged his error and added the time on to the second period with no explanation offered for his timekeeping cock-up. Maybe he was busting for the toilet. I mean, when you've got to go...

With an hour left and Millwall still trailing, any doubts amongst fans about Bob Peeters were seemingly dispelled as the booming Belgian bagged a brace in nine minutes to spark delirious scenes in the Priestfield away enclosure.

First he turned neatly in the area with his back to goal - almost Cascarino-like - to strike the equaliser and when he struck a beautiful left foot shot across The Gill's six yard box, Millwall were looking good for a first win over the Kent club in seven attempts - and top of the league.

Moments later Millwall had the chance to seal the points - and a memorable hat-trick for Peeters.

Gills defender Nyron Nosworthy's mis-timed diving header fell at the feet of Neil Harris who moved into the box with only 'keeper Vince Bartram to beat - and Peeters at his side ready to slot into an empty net.

Like all self-respecting strikers, Harris had built his

reputation on being greedy. To want every penalty, free kick and two-inch tap-in was the stock-in trade of the ruthless frontman. It was a mentality, taught by Lions' assistant manager Steve Harrison to Teddy Sheringham back in 1990, that turned Sheringham from a 20 goal-a-season striker into a 38 one.

Harris had buried dozens of similar chances and will, understandably, have not given a thought to squaring to Peeters. Had it been any other positioned player, they almost certainly would have done.

Harris shot, but the ball rebounded off Bartram's legs and to safety, much to the despair of the waiting Peeters.

Ten minutes later Gillingham striker Marlon King looped his side level and a miserable ending to what had promised to be such a glorious afternoon was complete when Nosworthy atoned for his earlier error by nipping the ball past the advancing Warner from King's pass.

Richard Sadlier's retirement was officially marked by an emotional tribute in the programme for the next match at home to Wimbledon, by which time defeat had once more been tasted on the road at Watford. In a feisty encounter that saw Kevin Muscat make his second appearance in the Millwall defence, the Australian full back seemed to hand the points to The Hornets with a rush of blood in the final minute of the first half.

Paul Ifill had equalised a Dyer opener and as Muscat dispossessed Watford's Webber in the half's final seconds, the stand-in Hornets forward took a petulant swing at the Millwall defender. Rather than ignore him and walk the ball out of his penalty area and to safety, Muscat stamped on Webber leaving referee Knight no option but to point to the penalty spot and red card Muscat.

Cox despatched the penalty and a third by Watford debutant Ashley Young right at the death settled it. Days after the match Millwall's parlous financial state was confirmed when chairman Theo Paphitis revealed the club had suffered losses of £4.7million. A perfect storm of the collapse of ITV Digital, reduced gate receipts and increased players' wages was to blame. McGhee insisted meanwhile that these figures would not affect his spending plans. Fans were understandably sceptical of this.

If those first two defeats of the season had Millwall fans feeling that the footballing gods had stopped smiling on them, it was nothing compared to what Wimbledon fans were going through. After ending their groundshare with Crystal Palace the previous season, the club had relocated to Milton Keynes.

In a saga that had started two years earlier, dismayed Dons fans set up AFC Wimbledon who, starting in the bottom tier of the non-league pyramid were attracting more fans than the second tier side.

Despite fervent opposition, the decision to relocate to Milton Keynes was approved by the football authorities and they started the 2003/04 season playing home games in the land of the concrete cow - after entering administration earlier in the summer.

Millwall were the latest team to capitalise on a club spiralling out of the division at a rapid rate with a 2-0 win courtesy of a Harris penalty and last minute Whelan strike and they made it two wins from two at home with another Harris spot kick sealing a 2-1 comeback win over Walsall in preparation for the eagerly-awaited trip to West Ham.

The Lions started on the front foot at Upton Park and Cahill should have given them the lead when good work from Peeters and Ifill on the left presented the Australian midfielder with what looked like the easiest of chances but his shot from the edge of the six yard box cannoned back off the goalkeeper's legs.

Predictably West Ham scored with their first meaningful strike when Connolly raced clear in the area and slid the ball past Warner and Millwall appeared to be heading for another fruitless trip east of the river.

Ifill smashed a shot against the Hammers' bar as Millwall pressed for a second half equaliser and the pressure eventually told when his cross was met by Cahill for what was now one of his trademark headed goals to send the travelling fans behind the goal berserk and seal a well-deserved point. The spirit shown at West Ham was worryingly lacking two days later when Millwall completed a unique sequence of playing five of the division's six teams beginning with W with a 1-2 defeat at West Brom. The match was all over midway through the first half thanks to goals from Koumas and Dobie.

October began with an encouraging home win over Coventry thanks to goals from Harris and Ifill but there was an increasing feeling around The Den that all was not well.

A goalless draw at Rotherham was followed by a numbing 0-1 home defeat to Preston where Mark McGhee's starting team selection had fans scratching their heads with Whelan and Peeters suddenly out of favour.

Rumours of fallouts between McGhee and Paphitis, the players and Archie Knox, and the inevitable name of Dennis Wise also cropping up in almost all of these conversations meant that when the club confirmed they had parted company with McGhee, there was little surprise. There was also no surprise in his temporary replacement, with Dennis Wise taking caretaker charge and immediately omitting himself from the team for a 2-0 home win over Sheffield United and a 1-1 draw at Burnley.

After a few years of relatively steady progress, so much had changed at Millwall so quickly. Dennis Wise was about to usher in an unbelievable new chapter in the history of Millwall Football Club.

Daydreams & Nightmares - Millwall FC in the 2000s - Part 1

15. Wise after the event

November 2003...
4 November – Channel 4's soap opera Brookside, on air since the station was launched in 1982, ends after 21 years; 22 November – England are rugby world champions after defeating Australia 20-17 after extra time; 26 November – the final Concorde flight touches down in Filton, Bristol where it is welcomed by the Duke of York...

Dennis Wise' caretaker tenure in the Millwall hotseat got off to an encouraging start. Despite opinion amongst Lions fans remaining as split on Wise as manager as they had been when he arrived as a player, as with Mark McGhee, results on the pitch were speaking for themselves. At least for now...

November started with a 1-0 win at home to Nottingham Forest, thanks to a goal on the stroke of half time from the enigma that was Kevin Braniff. The Belfast-born striker came through the ranks highly regarded and his form for youth and reserve teams earned him a first team debut at the age of just 17 at the start of the 2000/01 promotion season. He scored on that debut and looked destined for a bright future but quickly faded as McGhee's arrival coincided with the push for promotion and necessity for experience. After three years in the wilderness he now appeared to be finding his second chance under Wise and grasping it with both hands. Fans were often frustrated with a player that looked ruthless one minute and anonymous the next, perhaps not giving him the benefit of his still young years.

Braniff's goal settled a rather unremarkable match, brightened up by another Theo Paphitis masterpiece in the matchday programme.

Now seemingly lifted from the post-play-off gloom, Paphitis was back on top form, penning a piece criticising local rivals Crystal Palace for their somewhat creepy obsessive coverage of Millwall's latest managerial appointment. This allegedly borne out of Theo's opposite number at Selhurst Park Simon Jordan failing to sign Wise when Millwall went in for him. Referring to Jordan's club as "Crippled Alice", their ground as "Smellhurst Park" and dubbing them "Smellhurst Suburbanites", the piece, written with tongue firmly in cheek was all part of the pantomime being played out between Paphitis and Jordan who were in fact, good friends:

PEOPLE IN GLASS HOUSES...

The great thing about local rivalries is that when things are going pear-shaped at home, you can look over the fence and forget your problems by having a pop at your neighbour. Step forward our good friends at Crippled Alice, who devoted almost three pages of their match programme for their recent game against Ipswich (resulting in another home defeat unfortunately) to criticising Millwall.

In particular, they took umbrage with our decision to part company with Mark McGhee, suggesting in effect that because we don't attract as large attendances as they do, we have no right to harbour ambitions to better ourselves. From their perspective perhaps, having finished above The Beagles in the last two seasons, they probably can't understand how we can want for anything more. Indeed, after their recent run which has seen them win just one of their last 12 League games, it is understandable that they should come to view First Division survival as a cause for wild celebration.

At least their midweek Carling Cup win at Blackpool provides them with some encouragement that they'll be able to cope alright with Division Two. Maybe the fact that they do not own their own ground and are at the mercy of one Ron Noades as to whether they can continue playing at Smellhurst Park, or are forced to groundshare with Wimbledon at Milton Keynes, makes them so insecure.

To further slag off Dennis Wise, a player they tried to sign and who has won more than they could ever dream of, but who gave them the brush-off in favour of Millwall, shows what a small-minded little club they really are. The accusation that I made a knee-jerk decision is choice coming from a club for whom the words 'knee' and 'jerk' should be interwoven into their club crest. Funnily enough I bumped into Simon Jordan in a bar in Spain last week, and who should he be deep in conversation with but Mark Goldberg. I almost fell off my chair!

"Oh look," I said, "the man who almost wrecked Crystal Palace talking to the one who's about to!" Seriously, though, I hope Palace manage to stay up. Even if we're not in this Division to play them, they might be able to concentrate their spite at the team they really love to hate, Brighton.

In spite of what they might like to think, Mark McGhee left us on good terms and I wish him all the very best in his new job, especially if he gets the Seagulls promoted which will annoy the Smellhurst suburbanites even more.

On the subject of our managerial vacancy, the situation remains the same at present. We've had over 60 applications, and around eight of those are of a very high calibre.

We are determined to take our time and ensure that we make the right appointment. Dennis and Ray remain in charge until after the Norwich game. Things should start to become clearer over the next fortnight.

That more sensible last paragraph suggested Wise's temporary tenure was exactly that with the search for a new manager seemingly well under way, which was just as well as, after that 1-0 win over Forest, the honeymoon period appeared to be well and truly over.

Defeats at Norwich and Reading were followed by a drab 0-0 draw at home to struggling Derby. Yet by the time The Rams arrived at The Den, Wise and his assistant Ray Wilkins had been given their jobs on a permanent basis. It was a decision that certainly raised an eyebrow or two - especially with the 60-plus applicants for the post according to Paphitis. It can only be assumed that the Millwall chairman believed Wise and Wilkins could do a job but that the pair wanted the opportunity to do it with the full backing of the board.

Managerial matters settled, the month appeared to be ending on a brighter note when Wise's Lions travelled to second-bottom Bradford and goals from Cahill and Chadwick sent them in 2-0 up at the break.

But they capitulated alarmingly in the second half, allowing the Yorkshire side to comeback and nick all three points courtesy of a last-minute goal from Branch.

Flame-haired frontman Nick Chadwick had been acquired on loan from Everton and looked a promising addition to The Lions' attack, but it was the defence that was causing concern.

It was a relief then to start December with two clean sheets at home to promotion-chasing Norwich and Ipswich, but equally frustrating that Millwall were unable to score themselves, making it three consecutive goalless draws at

The Den ahead of the tricky trip to play-off hopefuls Cardiff in front of the live television cameras.

Another youth prospect made the trip to south Wales memorable for those Millwall fans that crossed border. Peter Sweeney was a wide man that had been earning rave reviews in the Millwall youth side and marked his fifth start with the 85th-minute goal that sealed an impressive 3-1 win over The Bluebirds, sending Millwall into the top half of the table ahead of the Boxing Day trip to Crystal Palace.

Over 4,000 Lions fans made the short trip to "Smellhurst Park" to face a Palace side down in 19th place under the stewardship of Ian Dowie.

A 14th-minute Neil Harris goal was enough to settle the match which saw Palace squander a host of second half chances - including a penalty, saved by Tony Warner - to prompt a pitch invasion and centre circle jig of delight from Theo Paphitis - no doubt purely for the benefit of Simon Jordan.

Another youth product that had made his way into the injury ravaged side that Wise and Wilkins had inherited was Marvin Elliott. The athletic midfielder had the finesse of Steven Reid and already fans were cautiously comparing the emerging talent with that of three years previously.

Millwall's little four match unbeaten run - and a very up and down year - was brought to an end in typical fashion however. Gillingham visited The Den as one of The Lions' biggest bogey sides in recent years. In nine league and cup matches between the two sides, Millwall had managed just two draws, losing the other seven. The impressive Chadwick looked to have secured at least a third draw for the sequence when he cancelled out Hessenthaler's first half opener, but a last minute winner by James helped the Kent club extend the run.

Millwall's home form had becoming worryingly wobbly.

With just one win at The Den since the middle of October, the next team to visit would be Walsall for an FA Cup third round tie and, if Wise and Wilkins couldn't find the remedy for The Lions' home failings, it would mean another early exit.

Fortunately, Millwall fans wouldn't have to worry about exiting the FA Cup for quite a while...

16. Never saw that coming...

January 2004...
6 January - The coroner's inquest into the death of Diana, Princess of Wales and her lover Dodi Al-Fayed is officially opened; The Daily Mirror publishes the blacked out portion of a letter wherein Diana, Princess of Wales alleged that someone was trying to kill her; 13 January - 57-year-old serial killer Dr. Harold Shipman is found dead in his cell one day prior to his fifty-eighth birthday following his suicide by hanging...

When Jorge Leitao gave Walsall a twelfth-minute lead in the FA Cup third round tie at The Den a wave of discontent and sighs of *"Here we go again"* swept around the chilly, sparsely populated stadium. Less than 7,000 had turned up to see what was looking like the end of Millwall's 2003/2004 FA Cup campaign at its earliest possible juncture. The attendance spoke volumes of Lions fans' acceptance of yet another home failure, and the increasing apathy for what was once one of the main dates on the footballing calendar. Even when goals from Braniff and Cahill reversed the scoreline going into the break and Millwall held out for an unlikely win, there was still almost a virtual collective shrug of the shoulders when referee

Beeby brought the match to an end. Years of disappointing cup draws when fans hoped for a big name to have a go at was replicated in the draw for round four when Millwall's numbered ball was pulled out after non-league Telford Utd. They were a side with a strong pedigree for giant-killing in the competition and a trip to play them in their back yard did little to inspire Lions fans who may have been tempted to consider the tie as a likely route to the latter stages of the competition. Millwall's football was frustratingly inconsistent, even by Millwall standards. Goals were being leaked at one end and even when they managed to keep a clean sheet, they were unusually shot-shy at the other. But two new faces would change all that, and send Millwall on a fifteen match run that would see them lose just once, provide their fans with one of the most memorable days in their history and exact a little bit of revenge that had been almost 70 years in the making...

After a goalless draw at promotion hopefuls Wigan, Millwall unveiled the first of two new signings for the home match with another team harbouring Premier League ambitions in Sunderland.

Danny Dichio was a well-travelled striker who had scored goals for QPR, Sampdoria, West Brom - and Sunderland. The tall, athletic front-man arrived on loan from WBA to replace the unlucky Nick Chadwick who had returned to Everton after an injury that required surgery. He made an immediate impact, scoring both goals to wipe out Stewart's Sunderland opener.

It was a match that was to lead to the second new arrival on loan in answer to an injury. Goalkeeper Tony Warner was expected to be out for at least six weeks after aggravating an old neck injury in the club's weights room and the experienced Andy Marshall was brought in just in time for the trip to Crewe who were beaten thanks to another Dichio double - the second being the last-minute winner -

and he made it five in three matches with the goal in the 1-1 draw at home to Stoke. The weather had seen the Telford trip postponed twice and meant that whoever won it would go straight into the fifth round match just four days later - at home to Burnley.

Pessimism was still the order of the day amongst the Millwall fans that made the midweek trip to Shropshire. They knew only too well the risk of thinking about a possible place in the last eight of the FA Cup with two seemingly winnable ties in four days. With the Telford pitch finally dry after resembling "a beach when the tide was coming in" as Wise described it, Paul Ifill took full advantage with a typical long range effort in the 37th minute that skimmed along the surface from 25 yards and deflected into the net, seemingly off the toe of a Telford defender or Danny Dichio. Either way, Ifill was accredited with the goal and Millwall were on their way. Telford had used the build-up to the match to try some typical underdog psychology but The Lions were impressively focussed and Wise - who had started a match for the first time since taking over from McGhee - secured a comfortable 2-0 win and set up a big day at The Den.

A surprisingly low crowd of just over 10,000 turned up to see if Millwall could earn themselves a place in the FA Cup quarter finals for the first time since 1985. Dennis Wise's programme notes thanked Theo Paphitis "for putting his hand in his pocket" to allow the club to make the Danny Dichio signing permanent.

As soon as it appeared that the addition of Dichio on loan was proving a success, with the striker in amongst the goals from day one, fans assumed his parent club West Brom would recall him, satisfied the player had regained his form and was ready to rejoin their promotion battle.

Not so!

Dichio's parting shot to the Midlands club was to paint a somewhat miserable picture of life at The Hawthorns: *"Morale there is very low, it's been like that for a while. It surprises me how they get results every week..."*

Manager Gary Megson had built himself something of a reputation for his methods of player discipline and proved he wasn't afraid to make enemies along the way if results were right. The two had clearly fallen out because with only three defeats in their previous 18 matches and in second place in the table, something must have been going right.

Fortunately, Millwall were to gain from Megson and Dichio's failure to see eye to eye but they had an equally formidable managerial opponent to overcome if they were to advance any further in the FA Cup.

Stan Ternent had initially been somewhat unfairly labelled a "typical dour Burnley boss" in some ignorant quarters and must have been revelling in proving them wrong. His side had a reputation for playing slick, incisive football and, with Premier League promotion ambitions stalling, they must have had an eye on the FA Cup to boost their season and bring just rewards for their brand of football - which would, eventually, see them in the top flight.

Sir Alex Ferguson once said that Dennis Wise could start an argument in an empty room. This was a typical Fergie backhanded compliment. The wily Scot rarely commented - positively or negatively - on any player that he didn't rate and, perhaps, would have happily had in his team.

Sir Alex famously managed with a siege mentality, a no-one likes us of his own engineering. Wise was in that mould. A player you'd hate to face, but would have in the trenches with you. The only problem being he might have a job seeing out of that trench.

Wise's real gift was to influence the opposition, to force

them to change their tactics purely because of him. They regularly felt, to their demise, that the best approach was to focus on him, distract him and allow that to take the impetus out of the opposition. Some ignorant footballing purists assumed, based on his Crazy Gang origins, Wise was nothing more than a pub player who ran around like a headless chicken, playing every trick in the book, conning referees and going to any lengths to get results.

There was a reason why that Wimbledon team was so successful and it was down to a lot more than mere Sunday league style gamesmanship. Stan Ternent fell in to the trap.

From the kick-off, it kicked off. But only from one side. Burnley had clearly decided to abandon their usual style of play and target Wise at every opportunity. The ploy can only have been to take out Millwall's lynchpin and secure at least a replay, or, hopefully nick a win against a depleted Millwall side down to ten men after Wise had been goaded into retaliating and sent off. Here was the beauty of the managerial version of Dennis Wise and this Millwall side that he had transformed so rapidly since his rather underwhelming first month in charge.

Wise wasn't the lynchpin of this side. When he played - and his rare recent inclusion coming in cup games only was clearly intended - he was a diversionary tactic.

In the one-off nature of cup football, most teams are less risk averse and looked to get the result by a different approach than they would normally employ for league football. Telford had tried the wind-up method, with their build up comments clearly intended to get Wise going after revenge. But while Telford eyes were on Wise, the rest of the team was going quietly about its business. The same scenario was playing out against Burnley.

While The Clarets were going all out to see Wise's claret, he happily kept them busy - and frustrated - by taking every kick up in the air, every shove and every off-the-ball dig with that familiar cheeky schoolboy grin on his face, at one point playfully ruffling the hair of one of his assailants.

Ternent's plan backfired fully as early as the eleventh minute when experienced referee Howard Webb had clearly cottoned on to what was going on. Burnley's Paul Weller shoved Wise in the head off the ball and was given a straight red.

Meanwhile, Millwall were dominating the match and only bad luck and good goalkeeping prevented them from taking a handsome lead into half time. A stunning left foot Ifill strike was tipped over the bar by Jensen as The Lions poured forward.

The risk of dominating so much without scoring is of course the breakaway goal and it looked like Burnley were going to snatch an undeserved first half lead when striker Ian Moore found himself with only Willy Gueret to beat, but the French stopper saved Moore's shot with his legs and almost immediately after at the opposite end a stunning Harris volley skimmed the Burnley bar to send the sides in at the break deadlocked at 0-0.

It was more of the same in the second half as Dichio worked tirelessly to unlock an increasingly tiring Burnley back line and he was rewarded in the 70th minute when he met an inch perfect cross from Muscat on the run to power what was becoming a trademark header into the back of the net. Muscat's cross came after the ball was played to him by Tim Cahill, following yet another dazzling run by the Australian midfielder. Cahill was having one of his best games for The Lions and appeared rejuvenated under Wise.

There was plenty of time for Millwall to increase their advantage but once again the magnificent Jensen in the Burnley goal thwarted their efforts and, with the final minute of the match ticking down, those saves looked to have proved vital when Alan Moore had the goal at his mercy but his header flew wide of the post, to the obvious relief and surprise of Darren Ward who he had managed to elude to secure what looked like a certain equaliser.

The final whistle blew and Millwall were into the last eight of the FA Cup where possible opponents included Premier League Manchester United, Arsenal, Fulham and Portsmouth - where Pompey had a certain Teddy Sheringham playing for them. There were two teams from the same division as Millwall in the draw - Sunderland and Sheffield United - and one third tier representative in Tranmere Rovers.

Obviously most teams would have been totally in favour of drawing Tranmere, but Millwall fans would have been a little more wary of the Wirral side.

Back in 1990, Millwall had the opportunity of a League Cup run to distract them from a miserable top flight season that would end in relegation. They appeared to be in command of their tie away to Tranmere, overturning an early deficit to lead 2-1 at the break but capitulated badly in the second half and lost 2-3.

So it was with trepidation that Lions fans watched the draw being made, torn between almost certainly going out with a shot at Arsenal or Manchester United, or the chance of a semi final place facing one of the sides outside the top flight at The Den.

It was Tranmere, but it was at The Den, where, despite Rovers' giantkilling exploits, The Lions would surely be too much for them, Rovers having won through to this stage with home advantage in the previous round win over Swansea.

More worrying however perhaps was that they had fought their way to this stage from the first round with wins away to Bolton and Luton on the way. Millwall's first post-war appearance in the FA Cup final four was by no means a formality. The match would be shown live - as were all of the four ties - but before it, Wise had to refocus his players' minds on league football, which it seemed they hadn't played in ages.

If fans were concerned that the players' minds would be occupied by the cup run, they needn't have worried.

A rare win at Preston courtesy of goals from Ifill and Cahill saw Millwall leapfrog the Lillywhites from 11th to 9th and back-to-back home wins against Rotherham and Burnley saw them suddenly in amongst the play-off places.

Both home wins had been immensely satisfying. Wise played himself in the Rotherham match, probably expecting a similar approach to that of Burnley in the cup game but it looked like the visitors had managed to snatch a point when a last minute penalty cancelled out Harris' first half opener, only for Cahill to pop up with the winner at the death.

The 2-0 win over Burnley came courtesy of goals from Sweeney and Ifill, sealing a comfortable three points.

The build-up to the quarter final saw Millwall travel to what could have been their last eight tie - Sheffield United away - and the 1-2 defeat wasn't ideal but the upturn in league form almost gave Lions fans some sort of insurance policy against cup heartache. If they were to become Tranmere's latest scalp, at least they had a shot at promotion with the league table looking very encouraging...

Nationwide League Division 1 - Mar 3rd 2004	P	W	D	L	F	A	PTS
1. Norwich	33	18	10	5	50	27	64
2. West Brom	34	17	10	7	70	36	61
3. Wigan	33	15	12	6	53	27	57
4. Sheff Utd	34	16	7	11	63	55	55
5. West Ham	33	13	14	6	58	44	53
6. Ipswich	34	15	8	11	58	45	53
7. MILLWALL	**34**	**14**	**11**	**9**	**61**	**47**	**53**

Daydreams & Nightmares - Millwall FC in the 2000s - Part 1

Daydreams & Nightmares - Millwall FC in the 2000s - Part 1

17. We're all going on a European tour...

March 2004...
11 March - Support for the Conservatives and Labour is equal at 35% for the second time in nine months, raising the spectre of a hung parliament at the next general election which is expected within a year; Al-Qaeda bombings on Cercanías trains in Madrid, Spain, kill at least 192 people; 31 March - Arsenal become the first team to complete 30 matches unbeaten at the start of a league season...

A sell-out Den nervously assembled to see if their side could seal a place in the last four of the FA Cup for the first time since 1937 when they had been denied a final appearance in controversial circumstances by top flight Sunderland.

The match began in a similar vein to the previous round encounter with Burnley, although rather than try to kick their way to a replay, Tranmere seemed to employ the more sensible tactic of containment, allowing Millwall possession without it coming to much harm. Although the rough stuff, when it did come, was once again aimed at Wise who sustained a nasty gash to the leg that required stitches afterwards,

With the game entering its final fifteen minutes, home fans

were becoming increasingly anxious about a possible trip to Tranmere where the underdogs, who had such a formidable home record, would almost become favourites. In the 76th minute, a move not dissimilar to the one that led to the winner against Burnley at a similar stage of the match saw Tim Cahill this time look to meet a Muscat cross. Time seemed to freeze as over 14,000 Millwall fans waited for the customary salmon-like rise of the Aussie midfielder and the bulging net as a result of another one of his famous headers.

Instead, under the challenge of Ryan Taylor, Cahill crumpled to the deck and referee Neale Barry pointed to the spot. The jubilant home fans celebrated not just what was almost certainly the match-winning spot-kick, but a trip to one of the country's finest stadiums to watch their team battle it out for a place in the final of the most famous cup competition in the world. A match almost 70 years in the making.

For the first time that season - and in that cup run - complacency had crept into the Millwall fans' makeup, and, as is often the case, they paid the price.

Muscat placed the ball on the spot and smashed it reassuringly down the centre of John Achterberg's goal.

The legendary *Saint and Greavsie* TV show from the 1980s once did a study of penalties to test Greaves' theory that placement to either side was less effective than simply drilling the ball down the middle, with the 'keeper almost always choosing to dive to either his left or right. Of course, the psychology opposing this is that you're kicking it at the goalkeeper. Greaves's findings weren't scientifically conclusive, but there was a strong support for the theory which Muscat adhered to.

In line with the thinking, Achterberg started to dive to his right, but slightly early, allowing him time to see the ball aimed centrally and to use an outstretched left hand to push it to safety over the bar. Millwall's chance had gone. Buoyed, Tranmere went in search of a winner and Millwall hearts were in mouths on two occasions as the visitors' tricky Canadian winger Hume came close. The final whistle was almost met with relief that their side were still in the tie.

The fact that a home league match with what was now a promotion rival as well as a bitter local one had been simmering away on the back burner rather than at the top of Millwall fans' agenda was testament to how suddenly the cup run had gripped the club. But now the visit of West Ham on the other side of the Prenton Park replay was very much in Lions fans' minds.

A trip to cash-strapped Ipswich was next, where on-loan Tractor Boy's 'keeper Marshall was allowed to play as the stricken East Anglian side had failed to lay down any conditions to the loan. Millwall eased to a 3-1 win at Portman Road, goals from Harris (2) and Ward enabling them to swap positions with Ipswich and sneak back into the play-off places.

Neil Harris had undoubtedly returned to the sort of form he was showing before his cancer diagnosis and, along with Paul Ifill and Tim Cahill, had become revitalised under Wise who had somehow revived the class of 2001.

Wise's tactics were spot on for the trip to Tranmere and from the moment they kicked off they managed to quickly silence the home support by putting them under immediate pressure.

It paid off handsomely in the 11th-minute when a Robbie Ryan free kick from inside his own half found Ifill whose lay-off was nodded down into the path of Tim Cahill by Dichio and the midfielder flicked his side into the lead.

Still shellshocked five minutes later, Tranmere were

unable to dispossess a rampant Lions side playing head tennis around the edge of their area and when the ball finally came down it did so to Dichio who perfectly teed up Harris for a spectacular volley from the edge of the area to put Millwall firmly in control. The inevitable Tranmere fightback came, resulting in a goal just before half time and, whilst there were some expected nail-biting moments in the closing stages (Richard Sadlier was among the travelling fans nervously pacing the concourse to kill the final agonising seconds) The Lions held on for a famous win - with an unexpected extra prize in addition to a place in the final tantalisingly theirs.

With the draw for the semi finals pairing Arsenal with Manchester United - both of which would be in next season's Champions League and not needing the UEFA Cup place that an FA Cup win would bring, the winner of the other semi-final would automatically be awarded that berth. Now Millwall were in that tie, and just one win away from not only a first ever FA Cup final, but a place in a major European competition. The team standing between them and that historical achievement? Sunderland.

April 10th 1937 saw Third Division Millwall travel to Leeds Road Huddersfield to face First Division title-holders Sunderland in the FA Cup semi final. The Wearsiders had won the previous season's league title scoring 109 goals with strikers Carter and Gurney grabbing 31 apiece. Nobody gave Millwall a prayer of course and Sunderland were expected to ease to the final.

Millwall were no pushover however and had reached the final four with giantkilling wins over Chelsea, Derby and Manchester City with striker Dave Mangnall starring and the club's exploits earning them the media moniker of *"The Lions of The South"*.

Sunderland were given the fright of their lives...

The odds were stacked against The Lions from the start with the decision to play the tie in Yorkshire, much closer for Sunderland fans who unsurprisingly outnumbered Millwall's in the 62,000 crowd where just 11,000 tickets were allocated to Lions fans. Back in London, 20,000 watched Millwall's reserves play West Ham, getting Tannoy updates throughout the match.

Mangnall gave Millwall an early lead which prompted roughhouse tactics from the shellshocked favourites - much of which went unpunished by the referee who was to miss an even more crucial decision shortly after Millwall had taken the lead, denying them a certain penalty.

A succession of corners led to the equaliser for Sunderland on 30 minutes sending the teams in level 1-1 at half time. As expected, Sunderland dominated the second period from the whistle as Yuill performed heroics in the Millwall goal to keep them out, but they finally succumbed in the 69th minute when Gallagher made it 2-1.

If Millwall wanted further evidence that the officials were determined they were to return to London heartbroken, it was proven in the dying minutes when a second stonewall penalty was waved away and The Lions' dream of reaching the FA Cup final as a Third Division team at the expense of one of the greatest teams in the land was gone.

The scenario for Millwall in 2004, as they bid to exact revenge almost seven decades later would be very different however. Millwall had already beaten Sunderland home and away in the league and whilst, like the play-offs, that is a dangerously inaccurate barometer to use in football, there was a sudden air of confidence and expectancy in the Millwall camp that they were not only destined for the FA Cup final, but promotion.

Semi-final pilgrimages to the Old Trafford Theatre of Dreams were planned, and then immediately parked, with the much more immediate business in hand of the visit of West Ham. Millwall's cup exploits had seen them slip out of the play-off places, ironically to be overtaken by Sunderland, but with games in hand the top six was a very real goal.

This was as long as they could gain points from the sides above them who they would face in the coming weeks: Reading, West Brom - and West Ham.

Millwall's final match of March would go down in fan folklore as *"The Mother's Day Massacre"*. If Lions fans were in dreamland having seen their team reach the semi finals of the FA Cup, nothing could prepare them for what was about to unfold at The Den on Sunday March 21st, 2004.

Shown live on ITV's *The Sunday Match*, a sundrenched Den watched as Wise once again pulled the strings and allowed his exciting side tear their rivals apart. But it took a little while to get going.

Paul Ifill was felled in the area in the 17th minute and referee Jeff Winter pointed to the spot. Neil Harris stepped up confidently but, as with Muscat's penalty against Tranmere, whilst the 'keeper dived, and the ball was hit straight, Bywater in The Hammers' goal was able to save courtesy of his trailing legs and the chance went begging - much to the glee of the visiting fans behind the goal. Millwall continued to press but home fans couldn't help thinking that in what would surely be a tight encounter settled almost certainly by a single goal, their chance had perhaps gone? They couldn't have been more wrong...

With ten minutes to go before the break, the lively Ifill sent in a whipped cross from the left which West Ham defender Christian Dailly attempted to block, only to send it past his 'keeper and into his own net.

Within 60 seconds of the restart, returning Everton loan

striker Nick Chadwick sent over a booming cross from the left which was met perfectly by Tim Cahill to head home and make it 2-0. Moments later the second penalty of the match was awarded for a handball by Matt Lawrence and Harewood made no mistake from the spot to seemingly put West Ham right back in it. Or so they thought.

On 56 minutes Paul Ifill sent a corner into the West Ham box where Cahill was waiting on the penalty spot, before any Hammers' defender could act, the Australian midfielder had sent a stunning left foot volley into the West Ham net.

At 3-1 Millwall were in dreamland, but by no means finished and it looked like four as Harris raced away after an Ifill pass from just inside his own half. In a duel to reach the ball with the West Ham 'keeper, Harris won, clipping it over the advancing Bywater but as he looked to round the stranded custodian and run the ball into the empty net, he was felled leaving referee Winter no option but to award another penalty - and send Bywater off.

After Millwall's previous two spot kicks had been missed - and with Cahill on an historic hat-trick - it was the Lions' number four that placed the ball on the spot and looked to complete his treble and make it 4-1.

Sub goalkeeper Srnicek could only watch as Cahill's kick sailed passed him - but also over the bar.

With ten minutes left the impressive Chadwick was sent clear and composed himself before smashing the ball into Srnicek's net to give Millwall the 4-1 scoreline that their dominance deserved. But it should have been more...

Millwall's biggest victory over their old rivals since the 5-1 win in their Millwall Athletic days of 1912 really should have eclipsed that scoreline. Had The Lions been as clinical from the penalty spot as they had been with their other strikes, Lions fans could have gone into work the next day gloating about a 6-1 drubbing of their old foe. But nobody was complaining.

Two away league games now stood between Millwall and their date with FA Cup destiny. Another Cahill goal was enough to beat bottom club Wimbledon and a late Ifill equaliser at Walsall saw Millwall travel to Manchester with just one defeat in twelve league games and established in the top six.

18. Four is the magic number

April 2004...
19 April - Tony Blair announces a change in government policy: there is to be a referendum on the proposed EU Constitution; 28 April - Landmark office building 30 St Mary Axe ("The Gherkin") in the City of London, designed by Norman Foster, opens;

There was a very unusual air around the famous old stadium as Millwall supporters slowly filled their allocated sections at Old Trafford on Sunday April 4, 2004. The nerves and anticipation that would normally accompany an appearance in an FA Cup semi final were not in evidence. There was instead a distinct feeling of confidence, not complacency, but that this was a day that would, unlike so many in Millwall's history, end well.

Millwall's managerial team of Dennis Wise and Ray Wilkins had used their vast experience of such occasions to prepare their side to the minutest of detail and they too looked comfortable and confident in the prematch build-up.

Wilkins was a vastly underrated feature of Millwall's set-up. His calm and calculated approach was an ideal compliment to Wise's livewire demeanour and both personalities complimented each other perfectly and permeated into a team that was in turn exciting, lively but also professional and clinical.

Wise's opposite number wore the look of a condemned man. But then he was Mick McCarthy, whose facial expression often betrayed his mood. McCarthy had of course cut his managerial teeth at Millwall in what felt like eons ago. There were few thoughts among fans of any form of revenge for The Lions over Big Mick however. Time had long erased the hurt of his long drawn out departure for the Ireland manager's job which set about a chain of events that would see Millwall drop from Premier League promotion contenders to relegation back to the third tier eight years before. Defeat to his Sunderland side would however sting, but this talk was not being entertained as one of the biggest matches in Millwall's history kicked off.

In an understandably cagey opening, Millwall made the better start, and while the tempo wasn't quite as gung ho as had served them so well in the Tranmere replay win, they looked comfortable and settled and odds-on the first team likely to score.

The first real chance of the match however came for Sunderland when, after being awarded a free kick 25 yards out from Andy Marshall's Millwall goal, John Oster smashed the underside of the bar. The collective sigh of relief from the Millwall fans behind that goal reverberated around the mild Manchester afternoon air for as long as the crossbar seemed to vibrate from the impact of the shot.

It proved to be a worthy wake-up call for Millwall and, in the 26th minute the goal came that would be etched in Lions folklore for almost as much as its numeric appearance as its significance.

Sunderland were unable to clear their lines as Millwall pressed and Ifill was able to gain possession on the edge of the area. His shot was parried but only as far as Cahill who gleefully hooked the ball into the Sunderland net to send half of the stadium into raptures. As he wheeled away twirling his shirt above his head, Cahill cemented an image in the minds of Lions supporters of all ages that would be indelibly ingrained, and with it, the statistic of the day's date and scorer: Millwall's number four, scoring on 04/04/04 to send their team to the FA Cup final for the first time in their history and bury the hurt of that 1937 defeat.

Of course, few fans there that day will have been alive for both matches, but one Millwall fan was.

85-year-old Jack Stimson was 18 when he made the trip to Huddersfield back in 1937 to see his beloved Lions' hearts broken by that 1-2 defeat to Sunderland. Whilst ill health prevented him from being at Old Trafford in person, he was able to watch the match on television and fulfil his prediction of a Millwall win to erase the pain of 1937.

Sunderland huffed and puffed but with every passing minute of the second half the match became one of a double celebration of both Millwall's first ever FA Cup final appearance - and their European adventure.

The celebrations that greeted the final whistle rivalled those even of Boothferry Park, Hull in 1988 when Millwall celebrated promotion to the First Division for the first time. As with that day in 1988, tears were unashamedly shed. For one particular group of Lions fans, the memorable day was well worth the trip from hell.

When their coach ground to a halt on Tottenham Court Road just moments into their Old Trafford trip, fans Keith Lawrence, Mark Batt, Bill Cruikshank, Davey Lawrence and Darren Shaw headed for Euston Station to make the rest of the journey by train. After being told there were no trains and services were only starting from Milton Keynes, they decided to hail a cab. Parting with £155 for the taxi ride to Milton Keynes was particularly hard given that the driver was a West Ham fan but it enabled them to pick up a train service to Manchester and a second cab ride from Piccadilly to Old Trafford saw them arrive for the match just sixty seconds after kick-off.

If anything negative had to be taken from the day it was the injury to fullback Kevin Muscat. The daredevil defender had been seen as something of a lose cannon in his initial Millwall career under McGhee. His impetulant nature causing his side to concede needless free-kicks and lose his services to suspension. Now that loose cannon had become a huge part of Millwall's attacking artillery with his exciting attacking play and brilliant crossing adding an extra dimension to The Lions' front line. With his discipline channelled, he looked to be heading for a place in the FA Cup final that his performances in the competition had so thoroughly deserved. That would now be denied him, not through suspension as many would have guessed, but thanks to a nasty knee injury that ended his season.

With fans' attentions now turning to acquiring tickets for the showpiece final - which would see Millwall face Manchester United at The Millennium Stadium in Cardiff, it was easy to forget that their team now had eight league matches to secure their play-off place and the unthinkable possibility of a second appearance at the Welsh capital arena in May.

Players' attentions were clearly on making that FA Cup date as Millwall's league form suffered an understandable hangover in the next few games.

A 0-0 draw at home to Cardiff (rather appropriately) wasn't enough to see them drop out of the top six, but a 0-4 drubbing away to Coventry three days later was. Second placed West Brom arrived at The Den next and ex-Baggies man Dichio scored the goal that looked like propelling Millwall back into the top six, but a 55th-minute Johnson equaliser levelled the match - and Dichio's season was about to enter nightmare proportions.

In a see-saw encounter at The City Ground, Dave Livermore gave Millwall the lead immediately after the break, only for Reid and Johnson to give Forest the initiative by the 69th minute. By that time however, the scoreline was the least of Millwall's worries.

Five minutes before, referee Curson had showed both Forest's Wes Morgan and Millwall's Dichio straight red cards for an altercation that would normally have mustered nothing more than a stern ticking off. Curson clearly fancied being the centre of attention however, and with The Lions' subsequent appeal against Dichio's card and resultant suspension unsuccessful, Millwall would play the FA Cup final without two players who had been so instrumental in them reaching it.

Dennis Wise made no secret of his desire to make it a double success and voiced his consternation that his players' focus had slipped since their semi final win. Their four match winless run since that Old Trafford victory now meant that a play-off place was out of their hands. Defeat at home to Watford and then Reading in the space of four days meant it was now out of reach.

Millwall's form since their semi-final win had been disastrous and a third consecutive defeat (0-2 at Derby) in seven winless matches saw them finish the season in a disappointing tenth place, despite a last day 1-0 win over Bradford - courtesy quite ironically to a converted Neil Harris penalty in a season of missed spot kicks!

Sunderland meanwhile had been galvanised by their FA Cup exit and secured third place behind promoted Norwich and West Brom. The sting of missing out on a possible play-off match - possibly with Sunderland yet again - was compounded by the fact that the very same West Ham team

Millwall had humiliated just over a month ago had managed to grab a play-off spot - alongside a Crystal Palace team that had appeared from nowhere to pinch the sixth spot that Lions fans thought was the least they would end up with - Palace finished just four points ahead of Millwall.

The injustice of it all has no place in football of course. Millwall had lost just twice in the twelve matches they had played against the teams that finished in the top six, winning five of the other ten and, despite the often-debated difference of facing a side in the play-offs from playing them in the league which Millwall had so much bitter experience of, Lions fans would have surely felt they had at least a chance of facing West Ham or Palace in the play-off final. Playing Manchester United in the FA Cup final on May 22nd and then West Ham seven days later in the play-off final was the stuff of dreams.

The reality is only teams with huge squads like the Manchester Uniteds and Arsenals of the world can cope with fighting for honours on more than one front. Millwall's squad was tiny in comparison and the understandable attitude of its players to protect their once-in-a-lifetime FA Cup final appearance meant that their opportunity to follow it up with promotion to the Premier League was always going to be out of reach.

As Millwall watched the play-offs rather than participating in them, there was an odd feeling of disappointment at the season's end. A season that had given them a history-making FA Cup final appearance but denied them probably one of the best chances of promotion in many years.

Watching West Ham and Crystal Palace win through to that final almost made it feel like they had become the hors d'oeuvres in a cup final they couldn't possibly win ahead of the season's domestic main course conclusion between two teams Millwall had beaten easily. As hard as it was to feel disappointed, they did. Play-off reservations put to one side, Millwall fans turned the city of Cardiff into a sea of blue and white as the big day finally arrived. As a guest of Gary Lineker on the BBC's live Match of the Day coverage, lifelong Millwall fan and broadcaster Danny Baker startled the presenter when asked if he felt The Lions had a chance:

"Of course not!" came Baker's booming, laughter-punctuated reply.

"Millwall have won by getting here, this is a celebration for Millwall fans today, our FA Cup is done, winning isn't really the point."

Rocked, expecting a battle cry for his plucky underdog Lions to pull of the shock of the century, he tried to coax a bit more optimism out of Baker, who was unrepentant.

"I feel sorry for Man United, they've gotta win this thing, Millwall don't. We can relax and enjoy the day. No-one thinks we can win..."

It was a typical response from Baker who never liked to toe the line and Lineker was clearly a little flustered with the response that had broken out of the programme's prim and proper format.

But he was right.

Supporting Millwall has never been about merely celebrating victory. Sure, we'll take it when it comes, but, as Danny Baker rightly pointed out, May 22nd 2004 was a party for fans to mark another landmark in the club's history. One of the many banners that adorned the Millwall end said it all, immortalising the line spoken by Leonard Pierce's Grandad character in the first episode of *Only Fools and Horses*:

"He's a trier ain't he? Your dad always said one day Delboy would reach the top. There again he used to say that one day Millwall would win the cup..."

As was expected, once the celebrations were over and seats were taken, eyes dabbed at the conclusion of singing *Abide With Me*, and hopeful roars bellowed to urge their team on one last time before the referee's whistle started the 2004 FA Cup Final, Millwall's season of celebration ultimately ended with inevitable defeat.

Despite the absence of Muscat and Dichio, Millwall gave a spirited resistance to the constant threat of Cristiano Ronaldo who was torturing Lions' left back Robbie Ryan.

If Millwall fans had perhaps been slightly disappointed that their historical first appearance in the FA Cup final wasn't at its natural Wembley home, Cardiff's Millennium Stadium did at least offer an arguably better viewing vantage point. And it was something that led to a typical Millwall exchange as Ryan once more failed to stop the rampant Ronaldo.

As the breathless Irish defender regained his composure, there was a momentary quiet that occasionally descends on a packed football stadium, as the crowd awaited another United corner. A shout from the Millwall fans shattered the lull:

"F***ing kick him Rob"

Ryan was just a matter of feet away from the first row of fans and a wry smile filled his face as he heard the shout. He couldn't help but reply:

"I've gotta f***ing catch him first..."

In a perfect comedy moment, his retort was delivered at the exact moment Ronaldo jogged past him to take the corner, clearly hearing the exchange and giving Ryan a chuckling double-take.

Inevitably the Portuguese maestro was involved in the first goal, rising unchallenged to head home, just as it seemed Millwall were going to go into the break at an impressive parity. More frustratingly, the goal came as a result of a mix-up between Wise and Harris. With the cross coming in and Harris spotting Wise ready to deal with it, he shouted "Time!" believing his manager had the opportunity to compose himself before clearing the danger. Almost immediately, inkeeping with his vast talent, Ronaldo appeared from nowhere. Harris' shout of "NO!" was too late and Ronaldo was able to head the opener, with a despairing Wise aborting his initial decision to head clear before hearing Harris' shout.

The second half was routine for Manchester United, a dubious penalty despatched by Ruud Van Nistelrooy was added to in the 80th minute with the Dutch striker's second goal of the game. The fact that large numbers of the Manchester United contingent left the stadium before the final whistle - let alone the trophy presentation - spoke volumes.

The history books will show that the 2004 FA Cup was won comfortably 3-0 by Manchester United. However they will also show that Millwall did contribute to the legend of the competition when they brought on Curtis Weston as a second half sub who, at just 17 years and 119 days old, became the youngest player to appear in a final.

Many people browsing these records will barely register who their opponents were. Millwall fans who were there that day and experienced one of the most bittersweet yet historical and memorable seasons in the club's history will never forget it.

And now they had a European tour to look forward to...

NATIONWIDE LEAGUE DIVISION ONE
FINAL TABLE 2003/2004

1	**Norwich City**	46	28	10	8	79	39	+40	94
2	**WBA**	46	25	11	10	64	42	+22	86
3	**Sunderland**	46	22	13	11	62	45	+17	79
4	**West Ham United**	46	19	17	10	67	45	+22	74
5	**Ipswich Town**	46	21	10	15	84	72	+12	73
6	**Crystal Palace (P)**	46	21	10	15	72	61	+11	73
7	Wigan Athletic	46	18	17	11	60	45	+15	71
8	Sheffield United	46	20	11	15	65	56	+9	71
9	Reading	46	20	10	16	55	57	-2	70
10	**Millwall**	**46**	**18**	**15**	**13**	**55**	**48**	**+7**	**69**
11	Stoke City	46	18	12	16	58	55	+3	66
12	Coventry City	46	17	14	15	67	54	+13	65
13	Cardiff City	46	17	14	15	68	58	+10	65
14	Nottingham Forest	46	15	15	16	61	58	+3	60
15	Preston North End	46	15	14	17	69	71	-2	59
16	Watford	46	15	12	19	54	68	-14	57
17	Rotherham United	46	13	15	18	53	61	-8	54
18	Crewe Alexandra	46	14	11	21	57	66	-9	53
19	Burnley	46	13	14	19	60	77	-17	53
20	Derby County	46	13	13	20	53	67	-14	52
21	Gillingham	46	14	9	23	48	67	-19	51
22	**Walsall**	**46**	**13**	**12**	**21**	**45**	**65**	**-20**	**51**
23	**Bradford City**	**46**	**10**	**6**	**30**	**38**	**69**	**-31**	**36**
24	**Wimbledon**	**46**	**8**	**5**	**33**	**41**	**89**	**-48**	**29**

Daydreams & Nightmares - Millwall FC in the 2000s - Part 1

Daydreams & Nightmares - Millwall FC in the 2000s - Part 1

04/05
end of an era

Daydreams & Nightmares - Millwall FC in the 2000s - Part 1

19. Fifteen minutes of fame

June, July, August 2004...
2 June – José Mourinho, the Portuguese coach who led FC Porto to the UEFA Champions League title on 26 May, is named as the new manager of Chelsea; 24 June – England are knocked out of UEFA Euro 2004 in the quarter-finals by host nation Portugal on penalties; 6 July – The Queen unveils a memorial fountain to Diana, Princess of Wales in London; 13 – 29 August – Great Britain participates in the 2004 Summer Olympics in Athens winning a total of 9 gold, 9 silver and 12 bronze medals.
16 August – Boscastle flood of 2004: flash floods destroy buildings and wash cars out to sea in Cornwall...

Millwall fans should have had every reason to believe they could go one better than 2003/04. Not winning the FA Cup of course, but to finally clinch that place in the Premier League. The second tier had been rebranded yet again, now being known as The Coca Cola Championship and Millwall unveiled a new kit with a new sponsor. White goods brand Beko now emblazoned an all blue home kit and while the majority of Lions fans were oblivious to the significance of the change of sponsor, or even who they were and what they did, it did show the first indication that chairman Theo Paphitis' involvement in the club was slowly ebbing away. In his seven years as chairman, his profile had climbed quickly and was a regular on television and radio with a natural flair for both. As the new season started, he was about to embark on his first major television role, in the second series of BBC's *Dragons' Den*. The fact that his Ryman company no longer appeared on the shirts was seen at the time, by those that cared, as a progression from having the chairman's company back the club to a more high profile commercial brand supporting it. But it would soon become apparent that this was the beginning of the end of a major era in Millwall's history.

With the Premier League now entering its thirteenth season, that meant over 30 clubs had been relegated from it with the riches that even one season's television rights would provide. The imbalance of the top two divisions was really starting to take shape now with the clubs promoted from the third tier (now League One) with precious little more TV money than they had the previous season. Faced with larger wage demands from their newly promoted squad, and having to find exorbitant transfer fees and wages for new signings to compete at that level, it was feared that the competitiveness would quickly be sucked out of the competition.

Either that or clubs would risk their very existence to compete.

With the FA Cup final now a distant memory, the failure to win what looked like a highly possible promotion before that semi final win at Old Trafford had caught up with Millwall.

Tim Cahill had left for Everton in a deal worth a reported paltry £1.5m, But with only a year left on his contract, Millwall's hand was forced. Had they managed to keep him for one more season, he could have walked for nothing.

Two other members of that 2001 title-winning team also departed with Tony Warner signing for Cardiff and Robbie Ryan going to Bristol Rovers. Goalkeeper Willy Gueret joined Swansea, replaced by Arsenal stopper Graham Stack on loan. Other somewhat unremarkable incomings were ex-Chelsea man Jody Morris and Canadian duo Josh Simpson and Adrian Serioux. The latter two coming about following the club's summer tour of Canada.

After a goalless season's opener at newly-promoted Plymouth, the now customary home curtain raiser with Wigan at The Den saw Wise express his concern at the lack of transfer activity, rather worryingly admitting that the squad was no stronger in terms of numbers than the previous season and far more lacking in experience. Meanwhile other teams in The Championship had strengthened meaning the chances of Millwall bettering that 10th place finish of the previous season were looking unlikely from day one.

There was no doubt that the distraction of the FA Cup final ultimately cost Millwall at the very least a place in the play-offs. The fact that Crystal Palace were able to come from nowhere, after barely troubling the top six all season, to beat a very ordinary Sunderland and West Ham to win promotion illustrated perfectly the chance that Millwall had missed.

Would Lions fans have swapped that glorious afternoon at Old Trafford and day out in Cardiff for promotion at the expense of West Ham?

Now of course, thanks to that final appearance, there was another early season distraction: The UEFA Cup. Just to read Theo Paphitis' words in his programme column for that Wigan match was enough to have long-suffering Millwall fans rubbing their eyes in disbelief:

"We would dearly love to have a run in the UEFA Cup..."

when for them, it still didn't seem that long ago that they

were hoping Millwall would beat Chesterfield to avoid relegation to Division Four. The format of The UEFA Cup was that unseeded teams - which of course Millwall were one - would have to play a two-legged first round - avoiding the two qualifying rounds which had begun way back in the middle of July. The winners of that would progress to the group stage. The draw would be made at the end of August. But if Millwall fans needed a reality check, hopes of a European campaign were put into stark perspective as promotion hopefuls Wigan left The Den with a worryingly easy 2-0 win.

What was more disconcerting about that Wigan defeat was that it was the start of Millwall fans turning on Theo Paphitis. The relationship between chairman and supporters had been strained in the aftermath of the 2002 play-off trouble and subsequent membership scheme, but there was a certain amount of understanding and slack allowed, given how much Paphitis' hands were tied by Police and football authorities. The FA Cup run had healed the rift somewhat but now, after losing arguably their most prized asset in Tim Cahill, fans were becoming disgruntled at the lack of investment in the playing staff.

The assumption was made that the FA Cup run had filled the club's coffers, but it was a sorely misguided one. The 2002/03 season had seen the club make a loss of almost £5m with attendances crashing, partly due to the membership scheme. The FA Cup run had brought in roughly half of that. With players' wages and the size of the squad also rising and average attendances only just creeping above the 10,000 mark, £2.5m doesn't last very long. In fact, it's highly likely the club barely saw the cash.

Millwall fans had other ideas of course and vented their fury in Theo's direction as their depleted-looking team succumbed to a Wigan side that was laden with Premier League-bound investment.

Daydreams & Nightmares - Millwall FC in the 2000s - Part 1

To compound the rift, Paphitis confirmed what many now suspected: that he would be stepping down as chairman at the end of the season. He insisted that this was not a reaction to the fans' fury at the Wigan game but something that he had discussed and confirmed with his board some time ago.

It wasn't the perfect build-up to the next home match with newly-relegated Leicester who boasted top flight-experienced talent such as Martin Keown, Keith Gillespie - and ex-Lions' loanee Dion Dublin. Yet somehow, in typical Millwall fashion, The Lions were able to defy the pre-match odds once more.

With their two Canadian imports making their debuts, Simpson impressed with his exciting, neat and nippy play and Serioux brought a talent of a very different nature. As soon as Millwall were awarded their first throw-in in Leicester territory, the imposing figure of Adrian Serioux was thrown - literally - into action.

He unleashed an astonishing long throw into the Leicester penalty area which drew an audible gasp from fans of both sides. This turned into a roar from Millwall's as Jody Morris got the slightest of touches to it to edge it past Ian Walker in the Leicester goal and give Millwall a 37th-minute lead.

The win was sealed with a welcome return to goalscoring form for Danny Dichio and Millwall were on their way. Two more wins followed - both 1-0 - away to Coventry at home to Reading, where Dichio was on target ten minutes from time in both.

The month ended with the long-awaited UEFA Cup first round draw. Millwall could have been drawn out against such names as Lazio, Sporting Lisbon, Benfica, Parma, Feyenoord and Brugge - all of whom had huge European pedigree. This was the age-old cup draw conundrum of course. Did Millwall fans want a big name and almost certain exit, or a chance to progress to the group stage and the certainty of facing at least one big name. As it turned out, they weren't sure what they ended up with. Ferencvaros were reigning Hungarian league champions, which in the eyes of Millwall supporters, didn't really help much in terms of gauging their threat. It was only reasonable to surmise that the Hungarian top flight couldn't have been anywhere close to the scale of the English one, so the assumption was made that this was an even - and tantalisingly winnable - two-leg tie. It was also a trip into the unknown against a club which worryingly had an appalling reputation for hooliganism.

The build-up to the first leg saw the arrival of striker Barry Hayles but once again minds appeared to be elsewhere as Millwall slipped to a 0-2 defeat at Ipswich before the home leg of Millwall's European debut.

Another disappointing attendance - despite the match being shown live - of just under 12,000 watched Millwall make history with their first ever competitive European match. The Hungarians looked happy to sit back, with Millwall offering little for three quarters of a cagey encounter, until the home side were awarded a free-kick on the edge of the Ferencvaros area on 66 minutes.

Dennis Wise stepped up to take the kick and placed it perfectly out of the reach of the visiting 'keeper Udvaracz.

Suddenly the Hungarians were sparked into life and began to dominate, showing their greater experience in the competition. With just over ten minutes left they were awarded a free kick of their own in a similar position to Wise's, and, just like the Millwall manager had done, the free kick was struck low and accurately beyond the outstretched had of Graham Stack to level the tie and leave Millwall with a mountain to climb in the second leg.

There was a Hungarian hangover next in the shape of a

0-2 defeat at home to Watford which saw The Lions slump rather alarmingly to 18th place in the league, but preparations for the trip to Budapest were boosted with a 3-1 win at Derby - where Josh Simpson grabbed his first Lions goal and a 1-1 draw at Rotherham. As some Lions fans joked as they boarded their various modes of transport to head across Europe to watch their team, you can't get a better build-up to a trip to a forboding part of central Europe than an afternoon in Rotherham...

The UEFA Cup first round second leg tie that took place close to the picturesque banks of The Danube was anything but. Reports of violent welcoming parties from the locals dominated the news, relegating the easy 3-1 win for the home side to a mere sidebar. The 4-2 aggregate victory saw Ferencvaros progress to the group stage where they would play Feyenoord, Schalke 04, Basel and Hearts. Millwall's fifteen minutes of European fame was well and truly over.

With the benefit of hindsight, and given the trouble witnessed in the Hungarian capital that night, avoiding trips to Germany and Edinburgh and welcoming the Dutch to Bermondsey just two years after the scenes that followed the Birmingham play-off match was almost certainly a blessing.

Trouble aside, the day-to-day humdrum of the Coca Cola Championship lacked the spark of European Competition and Millwall limped through the next four matches in uninspiring style. Lacking the energy of the side that had won through to the FA Cup final, October saw them remain in mid-table with wins over Nottingham Forest countered by defeat at Sunderland. A first win against Gillingham in eleven attempts where Hayles got his first for the club was followed by a disappointing 2-2 draw against bottom club Cardiff.

But there was still a bit more cup excitement to come.

Another benefit of their FA Cup and UEFA Cup exploits was a free pass to the third round of the League Cup. The draw for that round had, astonishingly after years of bad cup draws, seen Millwall drawn against Liverpool at The Den. Rafa Benitez's side eased to an expected 3-0 win but it was a spectacle witnessed by a packed Den that capped a remarkable calendar year of cup adventures for Millwall Football Club.

October ended with a 0-1 defeat at Stoke and Millwall without cup distractions for the first time in ten months, but seemingly going nowhere in the league. November would see the hotly-anticipated visit of West Ham to The Den where Lions fans were hopeful of another humiliation of their bitter rivals. Before that however there were matches against promotion chasing QPR away and Sunderland at home.

Barry Hayles was starting to show the goalscoring form that had seen him such a prolific striker at Stevenage, Bristol Rovers and Fulham and was unlucky not to score the winner at Loftus Road, his opener being cancelled out by a late Furlong goal for QPR. Goals from Wise and Livermore were enough to see off Sunderland and Hayles was on target again in a 1-1 draw at Preston, yet despite a run of just one defeat in their last six league games, three draws in those meant they were unable to get their heads above the halfway mark in the league table in time for the visit of sixth-placed West Ham.

The draw at Preston had seen the debut of striker Scott Dobie. The highly-rated frontman had been signed from West Brom in a reported £300,000 deal. Such was his reputation at The Hawthorns, two Dobie-dedicated Baggies fans passed up the chance to watch their own team, favouring instead to witness their favourite's debut for Millwall at Deepdale.

Dobie could have marked a memorable home debut against West Ham where he impressed with an all-action display that was almost capped by a goal when his second half header looked to have crossed the line but was scooped from under the bar by a Hammers defender. But his contribution was enough to help Millwall to another win over their rivals. This time it took just one goal to decide it, with Dichio scoring virtually a carbon-copy of the one that beat Burnley in the FA Cup fifth round the previous season. Muscat's inch-perfect 78th-minute cross was met by the on-rushing Dichio whose timing was perfect to head the ball past the hapless Bywater in the West Ham goal.

Ironically the month would end in defeat, first to Burnley, a Blake penalty twenty minutes from time settling the match, and then at struggling Crewe, undoing all the good work of the previous little run and leaving Millwall going into December right back where they finished the previous season: tenth.

Wise had used three different formations so far, which perhaps explained the inconsistency in results and form. Starting with a more traditional 4-4-2 system, he switched to a diamond formation and then, during November, a 5-3-2 which was scrapped and reverted back to 4-4-2 following that Crewe loss for the visit of play-off hopefuls Sheffield United.

It seemed to be working when a Mark Phillips goal had Millwall ahead going into the last fifteen minutes, the young defender scoring on his first start for the club. But old defensive weaknesses were exposed again as The Blades were able to score twice in the closing stages to leave a frustrated Wise wondering what formation to try next for the trip to Wolves.

As it turned out, it was 4-3-3 and it seemed to work as Dobie scored his first goal for the club and Dichio sealed the 2-1 win with another of his speciality late goals.

The formation seemed to be working a treat as Brighton were beaten 2-0 next at The Den with Dobie on target again and the impressive Paul Ifill grabbing the second. As one of the last surviving members of the Class of 2001, Ifill appeared to improve with every match. He tortured West Ham with powerful wing play that saw him virtually unplayable. It was becoming almost inevitable that he would attract top flight interest at some stage and, with Dennis Wise still keen to add to his squad, the temptation to cash in would be too great.

A Jody Morris penalty five minutes from time secured a useful point away to Leeds, but Wise strangely abandoned his new system for the Boxing Day visit of top-of-the-table Ipswich in favour of 4-4-2 again. But it paid off handsomely. Goals from each of Millwall's new strike-force of Hayles and Dobie, and Dichio adding another in a 3-1 win that easily ranked as The Lions' best performance of the season so far.

A year that had seen unparalleled cup success ended with the best league form so far that season. A stunning Barry Hayles hat-trick in a 3-0 win at Derby had seen Millwall win four out of their last five, scoring eleven goals and finishing 2004 in the top six. Had Wise repeated his magic of the previous season when some astute signings transformed the team from mid-table also-rans to promotion contenders? It was beginning to look like it...

Nationwide League Division 1 - Dec 31st 2004

	P	W	D	L	F	A	PTS
1. Ipswich	26	15	7	4	50	31	52
2. Sunderland	26	15	4	7	47	22	49
3. Wigan	26	13	8	5	45	20	47
4. Reading	26	14	5	7	36	25	47
5. Sheffield Utd	26	12	9	5	36	33	45
6. MILLWALL	**26**	**12**	**6**	**8**	**31**	**33**	**42**
7. West Ham	26	12	6	8	35	31	42

20. An offer you can't refuse...

January 2005...
5 January 2005 - Everton pay a club record £6 million for Southampton striker James Beattie; 8 January - The BBC broadcasts Jerry Springer - The Opera despite receiving at least 45,000 complaints; 26 January - Rodney Marsh, the former England national football star, is dismissed from his position as a pundit on Sky Sports because of a joke he made live on air concerning the 2004 Indian Ocean tsunami;

When Millwall youth product Alan Dunne gave his side a 16th-minute lead against bottom-of-the-table Rotherham in The Lions' first league match of 2005, things were looking decidedly rosy for Wise's men. With the match being the first of nine against sides in the bottom half of the table, here was a golden opportunity for Millwall to not only cement their place in the top six, but perhaps even make a run for an automatic promotion spot.

By the time those nine matches had been played, Millwall, who were suddenly a shadow of the swashbuckling side that had ended the year so well, had gleaned just nine points from a possible 27 and were right back where they had started.

The decline began just 90 seconds from half time in that Rotherham match when Butler equalised for The Millers and despite a second half shake-up that saw Wise sub himself off, Millwall were unable to get themselves back into the game and allowed the visitors to escape with all three points thanks to a 69th-minute winner from Scott.

There was something of a sigh of relief after the next defeat though. Exit from the FA Cup at the exact opposite stage of the previous season saw Lions fans that made the trip to the Midlands to witness their side lose 0-2 to Wolves shed few tears. The feeling was that this meant their side could perhaps rediscover that magic that had seen them go all the way to Cardiff for the final last season in the league this time instead.

Hopes were high of this in the next trip to Nottingham Forest where an opener from Hayles and another from Dunne gave them a 2-1 win and saw them back in the top six.

The third meeting with Wolves in ten matches however saw a return to the frustrating form that had plagued the team soon after Wise took over and at the start of the current season. A last minute Seol winner saw a side struggling down in 18th place, who Millwall had beaten so convincingly away in the league less than two months before, beat The Lions for the second time in two weeks.

Off the pitch, there were about to be some more wolves at the door.

During January, Theo Paphitis approached director and lifelong Millwall man Jeff Burnige about the prospect of him taking over as chairman. It was an offer Burnige simply couldn't refuse, even though it meant taking a huge personal financial risk. Jeff, like his father Herbert, was Millwall through and through. Had he turned down the offer, he knew he'd regret it for the rest of his life. He knew that he faced some financial challenges, but perhaps the size and urgency of them were a surprise even to him.

Back-to-back goalless draws at home to QPR and away to Gillingham saw them plummet down to ninth place. QPR had lost six out of seven at the turn of the year and Gillingham's debut spell in the high life of English football's second tier was ending with just two wins in ten and yet Millwall were unable to break either down.

It only reinforced the age-old gripe among Lions fans that their side always seemed to struggle against sides below them in the league.

A third blank - this time in a 0-1 home defeat to Stoke had some of the more pessimistic sections of The Den looking to see how many points they felt their side would need to avoid a repeat of the shock relegation in 1996.

Fortunately it wasn't quite that bad, but even when the run of one win in the first seven matches of 2005 did improve slightly with a 1-0 victory at Cardiff, it took a Dichio penalty meaning Millwall had now gone five matches without scoring in open play. The Lions were unrecognisable on the pitch since the turn of the year, but off the pitch Millwall's problems were only just beginning.

Millwall Holdings' six-month figures were released in the week following the Cardiff match and did not make for pretty reading. So much so that, by the time the grim conclusion of the report was made public, the latest Millwall fire sale had begun.

Striker Scott Dobie left for Nottingham Forest - just 13 weeks after signing - for the same £300,000 that had been paid for him, and it was made clear that, with losses of around £2m (a figure that would have been far worse without the £1.5m sale of Tim Cahill and the £2.5m yielded from the FA Cup run) he wouldn't be the last to go. The bottom line was, if attendances didn't improve, or promotion wasn't achieved, more sales would come. And so Millwall, after more than five years of relative feast, were heading it seemed for famine quite rapidly. With a wage bill of more than £8m, the prospect of flogging off the family silver was once again a part of every day life at The Den.

It was the first time in his eight years at the club that chairman Theo Paphitis had succumbed to it, proudly, steadfastly promising, season in, season out, that the club no longer needed to do it. Now even he had to concede defeat, and with the prospect of his departure from the club at the end of the season, a sudden wave of uncertainty that hadn't been felt in almost a decade swept through The Den. As if the financial situation wasn't bad enough, Wise also had to contend with an injury crisis that saw him take his side to Brighton unable to name himself, Hayles, Ifill and Muscat. He was also without the in-form youngster Alan Dunne who had been given a six match suspension after a last-minute sending off for violet conduct in the win at Cardiff. The resulting melee saw Livermore dismissed too, further depleting Wise's options. It never rains...

Of course, struggling Brighton were only too happy to take advantage of a severely under-strength Lions side and took all three points at the Withdean thanks to a last gasp Hart goal.

The Lions side that had for so long been bursting with experience was now blooding youth players more out of necessity than through their merits or in the interests of easing them into first team life. That is by no means a reflection on their abilities, but, as the club experienced back in 1979 when the successful FA Youth Cup-winning side was plundered in an attempt to get out of relegation trouble, it's not an ideal way to introduce them to the much tougher world of the English second tier.

Youngsters Phillips, Craig, Elliot, Weston and Quigley started the Brighton match and, when Phillips became the third Lions player to be dismissed in two matches when he received a second yellow card in the last minute, his replacement for the next match - a 1-1 draw at home to Leeds - was another youngster in Paul Robinson.

The fact that Robinson, making his first start of the season after being recalled from a loan spell at Torquay, scored the opening goal of the game told you everything about the backs-to-the-wall spirit at the club.

And the fact that Barry Hayles' return from injury was greeted with news that Danny Dichio was now injured and winger Josh Simpson joined the long queue into the Physio's room, told you its own story about Millwall's luck right now. If they didn't have bad luck, they'd have none at all.

Andy Impey was brought in on loan to try and bolster numbers and experience but, as is often the case with such signings who are surplus to requirements at their parent club, he was far from being ready to be thrown straight into a side that was now watching any chances of a play-off place fade fast.

The Leeds draw was followed by a Premier League-bound Wigan side completing the double with an easy 2-0 win and a Jody Morris penalty at home to Coventry meant that Millwall's sorry return in front of goal was now just one goal from open play in their last nine matches. To add insult to injury, it wasn't even enough to give them their first win in four, with Jorgensen equalising at the death for the Sky Blues. The return of the Hayles and Dichio strike partnership brought some well-needed respite, the month ending with a 3-0 home win over struggling Plymouth, but the writing was very much on the wall now. The club was beginning a familiar spiral.

Uncertainty had been heaped upon uncertainty when, in the aftermath of the 1-1 draw at home to Leeds, Dennis Wise went on record to admit that he didn't know if he was in the plans of incoming chairman Jeff Burnige. Further evidence of things unravelling fast was an exchange between Wise and a fan at the half time break at the Leeds match.

With supporter patience wearing thin, Wise reacted to comments from behind him and, before making his way down the tunnel for the break, approached fan Ron Wood. A reasonably amicable exchange followed (much to the relief of the attending stewards and officials) and the pair did eventually shake hands. But it was just another worrying sign that the atmosphere at The Den was becomingly increasingly toxic.

The postbag for the South London Press letters page was heaving with calls of support for incoming chairman Jeff Burnige, more misplaced demands for Theo to admit what had happened to "all the FA Cup money" (when the pages of the paper had explained this in some detail just a week or two before) and criticism for Wise and Wilkins' policy of bringing in older players.

At a fans' forum, Paphitis explained that every season's player investment was a gamble. For the first time in his eight years as chairman, that gamble looked to have backfired badly.

21. Up the creek

April 2005...
2 April 2005 – In a Premiership match between Newcastle United and Aston Villa, Newcastle teammates Lee Bowyer and Kieron Dyer are sent off for fighting each other.
5 April – Prime Minister Tony Blair asks the Queen for a dissolution of Parliament for a general election on 5 May; 7 April – MG Rover, the last British-owned volume car maker, is placed into receivership; Portsmouth appoint Frenchman Alain Perrin as manager, with Velimir Zajec reverting to his previous role as Director of Football.
10 April 2005 – James Vaughan of Everton becomes the youngest Premiership scorer as of this date when he scored in a match against Crystal Palace at the age of 16 years and 271 days.
15 April 2005 – Malcolm Glazer makes a revised bid to take over Manchester United.

Millwall had now entered one of those phases in their history where results had taken a back seat. Speculation and demonstration was the order of the day. April began with two depressing defeats at Leicester and Reading, before a bonkers battle at The Den with Crewe.

Hayles had given Millwall a half time lead and within five minutes of the restart, goals from youngster Marvin Elliott and Jody Morris had Millwall in the unusual position of being in control of a match and looking to run riot. Yet incredibly they managed to find themselves clinging on at 3-3 with ten minutes remaining.

It was left to another youngster, Ben May, to win the match with an 85th-minute penalty. Either way, it wasn't the best preparation for a trip to West Ham.

At Upton Park, the Hayles/Dichio partnership once again gave Lions fans a glimpse of what might have been had they been able to start the pair for the majority of the season. Hayles sent the visiting fans wild with the opener on twelve minutes and despite Harewood levelling, Millwall's best ever run against their rivals was extended with The Hammers failing to beat The Lions in six attempts.

Suddenly there was an air of calm about the place. Play-off hopefuls Preston were beaten 2-1 at The Den thanks to goals from Sweeney and Hayles and an early Morris strike at Bramall Lane caused all sorts of problems for Blades' boss Neil Warnock. With the 0-1 home defeat to Millwall putting paid to their play-off aspirations, Warnock was allegedly confronted in his office after the match by an apoplectic celebrity fan Sean Bean.

Meanwhile, in the sponsors lounge, a handful of Millwall supporters who had been guests of one of the match backers spotted Dave Bassett. The ex Sheffield United manager had been a guest of the club and was enjoying a couple of drinks while watching Jose Mourinho's Chelsea clinch the Premier League title on the big screen in the bar.

A typical down-to-earth football man, Bassett was happy to chat with the Lions supporters. But rather than smalltalk, the topics discussed were quite earth-shattering. He appeared to know quite a lot about what was happening at The Den, offering his sympathies for the approaching storm...

The programme for the final match of the season at home to Burnley became a bumper tribute edition to the outgoing Theo Paphitis. Never one to slip out unseen through a side exit, there were tributes from ex and current players and pages and pages of glossy recollections of the glory days.

Dennis Wise's own programme notes also read like a farewell of his own, even though the only official goodbyes in it were to players. Kevin Muscat would be returning to his native Australia, while on-loan goalkeeper Graham Stack would be making the slightly shorter jaunt back to Arsenal.

Wise's official departure wasn't far away however.

Within hours of the 0-0 draw with Burnley, discussions between chairman-elect Burnige and manager Wise resulted in Dennis Wise and Ray Wilkins leaving the club.

Wise, it was rumoured, had plans for one last all-out push at promotion, utilising Premier League players on one year deals, in a similar way that Bolton Wanderers had done. These short term deals were intended to prevent players from resting on their laurels and simply pocketing their wages regardless of performance or final league position. Bolton boss Sam Allardyce had managed to tempt some of the game's top players in the Autumn of their careers and keep his side in the top flight against all odds. Had he failed, whilst relegation would have been a blow, the club would not have been forced to keep the players or pay them off and the wage bill could be adjusted for the new lower level.

Apparently, thanks to their contacts in the game, Wise and Wilkins were already confident of making striker Les Ferdinand one of these signings, with at least half a dozen more in the pipeline. The plan would have swelled Millwall's already crippling wage bill, but would come with minimal risk as they could all be jettisoned at the end of the season. These plans - and the reality of the financial situation that the club now found itself in, couldn't have been further apart.

Having seen the parlous state of the club's finances in all its gory detail, Burnige could not possibly entertain such a risky plan and, what started out as discussions for next season, swiftly ended with club and coaches parting company.

Wise had been used to having a virtual free reign with recruitment and whilst Burnige was more than happy for him and Wilkins to continue, it would have to be under a very strict new set of operating rules.

The latest managerial departure spread more consternation amongst Millwall fans. They were now left with a threadbare squad, huge overdraft, rookie chairman and no manager. But they didn't know the half of it.

The Lions' new chairman had three pressing jobs to do: Raise some cash, reduce the wage bill, and most importantly, pay the wages for May. The latter was looking increasingly impossible as the club seemed to be spiralling into the financial mire at a worrying speed. At the eleventh hour, salvation came from a very unexpected source.

Burnige put a call in to the then Everton chairman Bill Kenwright. The pair had a good relationship borne out of the Tim Cahill transfer - and the fact that Burnige's wife was an Evertonian. The final instalment of the Cahill transfer fee was due at the end of August and so Burnige asked Kenwright if he'd consider perhaps paying it early. Kenwright was only too happy to oblige and didn't even ask for a reduction for early payment. In the cut-throat world of football chairmanship, Bill Kenwright truly was one of the good guys.

The job of balancing the books began with the departure of Darren Ward to Palace for just over £1m and Paul Ifill to

Sheffield United for £750,000, but this was just the tip of an iceberg that would have made the one the Titanic hit look like a swiftly melting kid's ice lolly.

Burnige was Millwall through and through and in terms of working for the club and knowing it inside out he had no equal. But being chairman is an entirely different proposition - especially of a club that you support and hold so dear to your heart.

As Jeff Burnige was about to find out...

COCA COLA CHAMPIONSHIP FINAL TABLE 2004/2005

1	Sunderland	46	29	7	10	76	41	+35	94
2	**Wigan Athletic**	46	25	12	9	79	35	+44	87
3	Ipswich Town	46	24	13	9	85	56	+29	85
4	Derby County	46	22	10	14	71	60	+11	76
5	Preston North End	46	21	12	13	67	58	+9	75
6	**West Ham (P)**	46	21	10	15	66	56	+10	73
7	Reading	46	19	13	14	51	44	+7	70
8	Sheffield United	46	18	13	15	57	56	+1	67
9	Wolves	46	15	21	10	72	59	+13	66
10	**MILLWALL**	**46**	**18**	**12**	**16**	**51**	**45**	**+6**	**66**
11	QPR	46	17	11	18	54	58	-4	62
12	Stoke City	46	17	10	19	36	38	-2	61
13	Burnley	46	15	15	16	38	39	-1	60
14	Leeds United	46	14	18	14	49	52	-3	60
15	Leicester City	46	12	21	13	49	46	+3	57
16	Cardiff City	46	13	15	18	48	51	-3	54
17	Plymouth Argyle	46	14	11	21	52	64	-12	53
18	Watford	46	12	16	18	52	59	-7	52
19	Coventry City	46	13	13	20	61	73	-12	52
20	Brighton	46	13	12	21	40	65	-25	51
21	Crewe Alexandra	46	12	14	20	66	86	-20	50
22	**Gillingham**	**46**	**12**	**14**	**20**	**45**	**66**	**-21**	**50**
23	**Nottingham Forest**	**46**	**9**	**17**	**20**	**42**	**66**	**-24**	**44**
24	**Rotherham United**	**46**	**5**	**14**	**27**	**35**	**69**	**-34**	**29**

Also by the author:
SOUTH BERMONDSEY HOMESICK BLUES
MILLWALL FOOTBALL CLUB

IN THE 1990s - Part Two

MERV PAYNE

Millwall Football Club went into the second half of the 1990s desperate to join the new, cash-rich elite in The Premier League. Blackburn had already proved that success could be bought and whilst they didn't have Walker's megabucks, which helped the Lancashire side go from the lower reaches of the second tier to Premier League Champions in a few seasons, a new chairman and fresh investment in The Lions' squad not seen since the 1987-88 Second Division championship-winning season meant Millwall's long-suffering fans went into the 1995-96 season with high hopes that their team would once again win promotion to the top flight.

They were in for quite a shock...

South Bermondsey Homesick Blues tells the story of Millwall's journey through the final five years of the 1990s and, as usual, it was an eventful one. From title hopes to relegation disaster, almost going out of business altogether and employing an arch rival's legendary player as manager, to the realisation of another Millwall fan's dream: appearing at Wembley.

Once again Millwall managed to cram into a few years what most other football fans experience in a lifetime of following their team.

Available at:

www.victorpublishing.co.uk/shop

also available in hardback, paperback and Kindle format at:

amazon

Also by the author:

AFTER THE LORD MAYOR'S SHOW

MILLWALL FOOTBALL CLUB
IN THE 1990s - Part One

MERV PAYNE

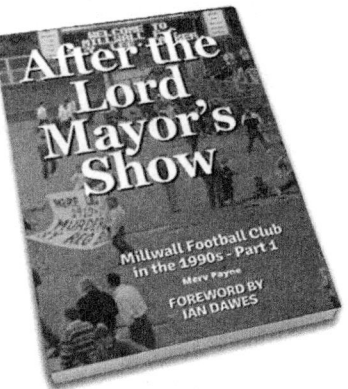

Starting the decade as a top flight club, Millwall were keen to regain that place after relegation at the end of the 89/90 season - and it would become increasingly important with the new world of riches that The Premier League would soon bring. Instead, their fans were taken on a 10-year roller coaster ride that included play-off drama, leaving their beloved Den, nearly going out of business and making a first trip to Wembley since World War Two, with plenty more in between. This is the story of Millwall's 1990s. It was life after the First Division, from the sublime to the ridiculous. Because we all know what comes after the Lord Mayor's Show...

Available at:
www.victorpublishing.co.uk/shop
also available in hardback, paperback and Kindle format at:

amazon

Also by the author:

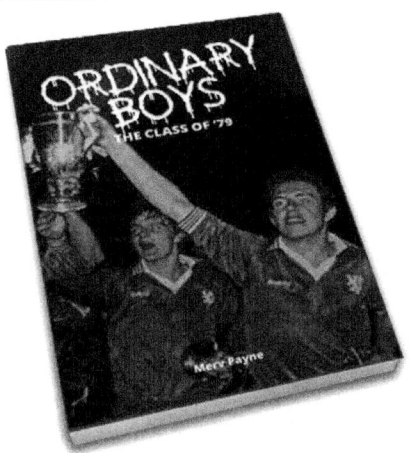

They were just a bunch of ordinary football-mad boys from the local estates, but together on the football pitch they were unstoppable.

This is the story of the Millwall team that won the FA Youth Cup for the first time in the club's history in 1979, but they were so much more than just a team.

An inseparable band of brothers, they defied the odds by not only beating some of the top teams in the country on their way to the final, they out-footballed them.

What was all the more remarkable was that they did it while the football club imploded around them under a constant wave of financial and other off-the-field troubles as it plummeted towards lower league footballing oblivion.

The club's dwindling fortunes would surely be turned around with the help of this new crop of brilliant young players graduating to the team.

Unfortunately, as we know, football isn't always quite as simple as that.

Available at:

www.victorpublishing.co.uk/shop

also available in hardback, paperback and Kindle format at:

amazon

Also by the author:

August 1988. The second Summer of Love. The UK wasn't basking in a heatwave, but the euphoric mix of acid house, rave and psychedelia meant that most were completely oblivious to the weather anyway. A year that had started like any other had blossomed in a feel good factor not experienced since the sixties. Love was in the air, house prices were up, unemployment was down and Millwall were in the First Division...

The Lions' appearance at football's top table for the first time in their 103 year history is probably best compared with Punk than Rave culture. Exploding on the scene and sticking two fingers up to the establishment, shocking their way to the top of the pile before being chewed up and spat out and then disappearing as quickly as they had arrived. But this was 1988 not 1976 and while their somewhat unwelcome arrival was no less dramatic and explosive than the opening chords to Anarchy in The UK, there was little bit more class about these boys as they slotted into the high life to the assured but no less revolutionary backing track of Voodoo Ray.

This is the story of a humble south London football club and its unique fans. How a team, built on a shoestring budget and made up largely of locals and boyhood Millwall supporters stunned the football world for a brief but beautiful time back in 1988 when football really was the beautiful game. For two years Millwall rubbed shoulders with the game's elite. Their fans, when they weren't raving in fields or warehouses, were gleefully gatecrashing a party where only the wealthy usually received an invite. There was delight and disappointment, triumph and tragedy, but what a ride.

During the late eighties, the drug of choice was Ecstasy, but for many, just following Millwall was enough, a truly natural high. With contributions from members of that historic Millwall squad as well as fans and opposition players and fans, this is a footballing tale that will never be repeated. Enjoy this trip, and it is a trip...

Available at:

www.victorpublishing.co.uk/shop

also available in hardback, paperback and Kindle format at:

amazon

Also by the author:

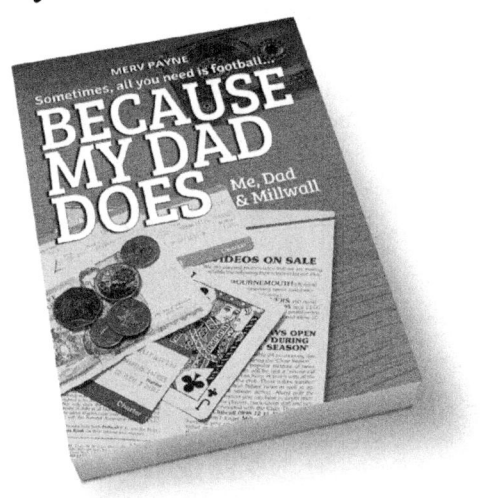

Merv was determined to forge a bond with his dad. It's usually the other way around, but he could tell from a very young age that he'd probably have to do most of the work himself.

After going to their first football match together when he was seven, a shared passion began that would last the rest of their lives - which is just as well, because they had very little else to cement their bond.

Merv's attempts to enhance this relationship through junior football almost had disastrous consequences, but their passion for football – and in particular Millwall – became the glue that held them together.

What Merv really wanted was to share unique, unprecedented success at Millwall with his dad – something that was very thin on the ground in the early eighties. What they both wanted more than anything was to see their team in the First Division for the first time.

Because My Dad Does is a nostalgic journey through the days of the terraces, following your team - with and without your dad - on teletext or the football special, and sharing a once-in-a-lifetime, never-to-be-repeated football season as father and son.

Available at:

www.victorpublishing.co.uk/shop

also available in hardback, paperback and Kindle format at:

amazon

Also available:
Millwall Who's Who:
A complete record of every player to represent Millwall Football Club: A Complete Record of every player to represent Millwall FC

A complete record of every player that represented Millwall Football Club. This essential publication for Millwall fans profiles every player who made a first-team appearance for the club since their first competitive game in 1886.

Have you ever wondered what happened to all those players you have seen come and go over the years?

The heroes and villains, the saints and sinners, the stars you have talked about for years after they retired and those who you instantly forgot.

Available at:

www.victorpublishing.co.uk/shop

also available in hardback, paperback and Kindle format at:

amazon

Also available:

Let 'Em All Come Down To The Den! An illustrated rhyming tale of the history of Millwall Football Club

Take a trip through the history of The Lions.

From their formation by the workers at Mortons Jam Factory back in 1885; through record-breaking goalscoring seasons, FA Cup heroics and unbeaten home records to agonising near misses, promotion to the First Division for the first time and Wembley glory.

Learn about the heroes and legends that have worn the Millwall shirt and discover fun facts about The Lions.

Let 'Em All Come Down To The Den is a rhyming tale of the club that parents, grandparents, aunts, uncles and older siblings can enjoy with their little Lions and will enable them to share and pass on their love of Millwall and why it's important to follow your team through good times and bad.

Available at:
www.victorpublishing.co.uk/shop
also available at:

amazon

Also available:

Millwall Wordsearch

A selection of Wordsearch puzzles covering the history, players and achievements of The Lions!

Available at:
www.victorpublishing.co.uk/shop
also available at:

amazon

Got a book in you?

This book is published by Victor Publishing.

Victor Publishing specialises in getting new and independent writers' work published worldwide in both paperback and Kindle format.

If you have a manuscript for a book of any genre (fiction, non-fiction, autobiographical, biographical or even reference or photographic/illustrative) and would like more information on how you can get your work published and on sale to the general public, please visit us at:

www.victorpublishing.co.uk

Victor
PUBLISHING
victorpublishing.co.uk